The
Senior
Minister

The Senior Minister

Lyle E. Schaller

Abingdon Press
Nashville

THE SENIOR MINISTER

This book is printed on acid-free paper.

Library of Congress Cataloging-in-Publication Data

SCHALLER, LYLE E.
   The senior minister / Lyle E. Schaller
      p.   cm.
   ISBN 0-687-37180-5 (pbk.: alk. paper)
      1. Group ministry. 2. Pastoral theology. 3. Big churches.
   I. Title.
   BV675.S33   1988
   253—dc19   87-28997
                                                              CIP

MANUFACTURED BY THE PARTHENON PRESS AT
NASHVILLE, TENNESSEE, UNITED STATES OF AMERICA

To: Leith Anderson
 James Barnes
 Peter Fath
 Dan Baumann
 Clayton Bell
 Claire Berry
 Virgil Bjork
 Ken Chalker
 Keith Cook
 Gary Demarest
 John Dodson
 Don Frogge
 Dick Hamlin
 Frank Harrington
 Curt Hess
 Don Jafvert

Dick Jessen
Dan Johns
Barry Johnson
Walt Kallestad
Gary Langness
Knute Larson
Ross Marrs
Don Morgan
Gordon Ralls
Barbara Riddle
Greg Robertson
Jeff Spiller
Gerald Trigg
Yvonne Trueblood
Gene Wells
Otis Young

Contents

Introduction

What is the best approach to improving the quality of the public schools? During the past half century the responses to that question have included: the requirement that every teacher have a bachelor's degree, the elimination of almost all one-room schools accommodating six or eight grades with one teacher, the reduction of lay control and the placement of more authority in the hands of the professional administrators, smaller classes, more money, new and better buildings, greater respect for teachers by the general community, compulsory kindergarten for five-year-olds, busing, more teacher's aides, higher salaries for teachers, improvements in the curriculum, radical revisions in the approach to teaching mathematics, reading, writing, and spelling, bilingual teachers, parents encouraged to enroll their three- and four-year-old children in pre-kindergarten experiences, a better and more supportive environment, and the improvement of the quality of the training of future teachers in the schools of education.

During the mid-1980s a consensus began to emerge that the key to a good elementary school is the principal. Literally dozens of studies, articles, and books have been published in the 1980s that argue that the principal is the most important single force in creating the combination of factors found in the best elementary schools. Similar reports have appeared emphasizing the role of the principal in secondary schools.

In a parallel manner a similar debate has been going on for at least two decades over what are the crucial factors in producing an attractive, vital, numerically growing, faithful, unified, obedient, and vigorous large Protestant congregation. Many people have endorsed the power and the importance of small groups while others have stressed the centrality of the Sunday school or the importance of music or the value of adequate physical facilities for worship, education, and fellowship or the role of the laity in planning and decision making or a high quality children's program.

Smaller numbers have lifted up the critical need for adequate off-street parking or the contribution made by placing the highest priority on missions or in sending a dollar away for every dollar spent locally or the importance of a team of highly competent, cooperative, committed, and productive program staff members or the value of a strong disciplining program for new members. Others have argued in favor of minimizing any references to the denominational affiliation while on the other side of that fence are those who contend a jackass is the only creature in God's creation that denies its heritage.

Likewise some observers argue in favor of a high degree of homogeneity within the membership and/or staff while others contend that a heterogeneous staff is the only effective response to the inevitability of a high degree of heterogeneity among the members.

It is easy to find those who are absolutely convinced that excellent biblical preaching is at the heart of the effective and attractive large church while others contend the teaching ministry is more important than preaching.

A large number of people claim that to become a large church in today's world requires a right-of-center theological position while others dismiss that claim by pointing to the scores of very large congregations that are clearly on the left half of the theological spectrum.

When taken together, all these claims argue against a single factor analysis. If, however, it is possible to isolate one factor, this observer's experiences suggest it is the senior minister.

This book is based on the assumption that the most critical single factor in determining the effectiveness, vitality, morale, attractiveness, numerical growth or decline, community image, and outreach of the large congregation is the senior minister. That is not to suggest the competence, gifts, personality, and initiative of the senior minister are the only factors. It is only one among many different influences that affect the life and ministry of the large church, but it is more influential than any other one item on the long list of forces.

Some readers may object this places a heavy burden on the senior minister. That misses the point. One of the most difficult challenging and rewarding assignments in our society is that of the high school physics teacher who has the responsibility to make a difficult subject into a fascinating exploration of new facts and ideas for teenagers, many of whom do not display a high level of self-motivation. To state that as a fact of life is not placing a burden on that teacher. It is simply confirming a self-evident reality. Likewise this emphasis on the centrality of the senior minister's role does not make it a burden. This emphasis is simply recognizing the reality of the situation. Any attempt to minimize the influence of the senior minister's role is a deception that seeks to distort or deny reality.

This book is about the role and responsibilities of the senior minister in the large congregation. That requires a definition of terms. First of all, the term "senior minister" is used here as a synonym for such increasingly popular titles as "head of staff" or "directing minister." That assumes the staff includes one or more additional program persons, either part-time or full-time, *in addition* to the choir director and/or organist. This definition also assumes the senior minister has the reponsibility for the oversight or supervision of other program staff members in addition to the secretarial, bookkeeping, and custodial help. In many congregations the program staff consists of two individuals, the senior pastor and the associate minister. Increasingly, however, the trend is to expand the staff with part-time lay specialists and to reduce the number of full-time clergy. Typically the senior minister has the primary responsibility for deciding on the configuration of the staff team and an influential voice in selecting new members for that team.

More and more churches are duplicating the military

model of unit commander and an executive officer with a staff headed by the preaching minister and the executive minister. In many of these arrangements a large share of the traditional responsibilities of the senior minister is assigned to the executive minister including oversight of the rest of the staff.

If the year is 1950, the definition of a large church might be the congregation averaging three hundred or more at Sunday morning worship, and in many of these the pastor was the only professional program person on the staff. As life has become more complicated, as the membership has become more diverse and as churches have become more sensitive to the differences among people, the ministry, program, and outreach of the large church has become far more complex. One common result is a larger program staff.

The result of that increased complexity and larger staff is that hundreds of congregations averaging 180 to 240 at worship now have one or more paid program specialists on the staff in addition to the pastor. In several denominations the policy is to add a second program specialist to the staff of the new congregation soon after the average attendance at worship exceeds 135. The obvious reason for this policy is to maintain the momentum of rapid numerical growth. If it took two years for that new mission to reach an average attendance of 135, the goal is to reach 250 before the end of the fifth year.

One result of these and other changes is that the number of senior ministers in American Protestantism has at least quadrupled since 1950. As the size at which a congregation begins to add program staff goes down, the number of multiple-staff congregations goes up. In addition, the emergence since 1960 of hundreds of exceptionally large churches has created a new set of models.

Another approach to defining the term "large church" is to think in comparative terms. If a large congregation is defined as one that has a higher average attendance at worship than four out of five churches in that denomination, this means all congregations from the former Lutheran Church in America averaging more than 205 at worship should be defined as large. Any United Church of Christ congregation averaging more than 150 at worship is in the top 20 percent in that denomination. Any United Methodist congregation averaging more than 133 at worship is among the top 20 percent in size and congregations averaging more than 215 at worship are among the top 10 percent in that denomination while an average attendance of 255 is required in order to be among the largest 20 percent of all congregations in the Lutheran Church-Missouri Synod.

As every black reader and most white or Asian readers will detect, this book is the product of an Anglo's experiences working largely with Anglo congregations in North America. Much of what is recommended in the following pages is taken for granted by black pastors. The black churches in the United States expect their ministers to be leaders, not enablers or facilitators, and the vast majority of black clergy accept that leadership role without any reservations. This is one reason why it is relatively easy for a black minister to serve effectively as the pastor of a white congregation while the list of success stories of white ministers serving all-black congregations is comparatively short. Another reason, of course, is that most black clergy have spent several decades learning how to survive in an Anglo culture while very few white pastors have even three decades of experience in learning how to function in a black subculture.

This is not an apology, but simply an attempt to state the obvious. Black, Asian, and Hispanic senior ministers may find useful insights and suggestions in this book, but they will have to be more selective in their reading than the typical white pastor.

Similarly this book is drawn almost entirely from experiences and research on congregations, both black and white, with male senior ministers. By 1998 the experience base should be sufficiently large and varied for someone to write a good book on the differences in roles between the woman who is a senior minister and the man in a similar position. All we know for sure at this point in history is there are significant differences. For example, it is not uncommon for the thirty-five-year-old male senior minister to have an excellent relationship with the fifty-nine-year-old woman who is the pastor's secretary. When a thirty-eight-year-old senior minister was asked to explain why she asked for the resignation of the fifty-nine-year-old secretary who had been on the staff of that congregation for more than thirty years, this newly arrived senior minister replied, "I already have one mother, and that's enough!" The deference pyramid may not be the same for the female senior minister as for her male counterpart in a similar church!

This book also is based on the assumption that the most frequently traveled route to becoming a senior minister is first to serve two or three pastorates in smaller congregations and gradually "work up" to the opportunity to become the senior pastor of a large church. That assumption is being challenged by a growing number of people. It is being challenged by laypersons on pulpit nominating committees who may limit their search to ministers who have served as associate pastors of larger congregations. As one member of the search committee in a 1,700-member church explained, "We are not looking for someone who will come and say, 'I've never been in a congregation as large as this one before, but . . .' We're looking for someone who will come in here and say, 'While I've never been in a congregation as small as this one before . . .' We're seeking a new senior minister who will challenge us with a larger vision of what could be. We don't want a senior minister with lots of experience in a middle-sized church who comes here to turn us into a middle-sized church so his experience will become relevant again."

Another group challenging the assumption that the position of senior minister should be seen as the top of a ministerial career ladder is composed of those who believe twenty years in smaller congregations may not be the best preparation for becoming a senior minister. Some members of this group argue that in fact it may be a counterproductive approach to preparing a person to become a senior minister. The typical small church trains the minister to react to the context and to the initiative of others. The large church wants a senior minister who will initiate and lead. The small church teaches the pastor to do it all. The large congregation needs a senior minister who will accept the responsibility for making sure everything gets done but expects others to do most of the doing. The small church teaches that the pastor should be able to do everything, to be a jack-of-all-trades. The large congregation needs a minister who can specialize in a few areas of ministry with a high level of competence and delegate to other skilled specialists many other responsibilities *and not feel guilty about not doing everything.* Smaller churches place a premium on relationships, expect much of the administrative and policy making to be done by lay volunteers and often assume the minister will spend 15 to 30 percent of the typical day on secretarial chores. The large congregation needs a senior minister who is an excellent preacher, a skillful administrator, who can challenge the laity to a greater vision of a new tomorrow and who is comfortable delegating secretarial tasks to a skilled secretary.

The small congregation rewards the minister who excels in one-to-one relationships. The large congregation needs a senior pastor who understands the value of relating to people in groups, rather than concentrating on one-to-one relationships, and can model that role for other members of the staff.

These are but a few of the differences that are causing what appears to be an increasing number of church leaders to question the wisdom of the "move up the ladder" road to becoming a senior minister. (This point is discussed at greater length in the first part of chapter 5.)

In summary, this book has been written on the assumption that the minister who spends ten or more years serving as the only program staff person in a small or middle-sized Protestant congregation and subsequently becomes the senior minister of a large church will experience considerable discontinuity. In addition, it also is assumed few resources have been prepared for the benefit of those who are following what is clearly a unique Christian vocation.

For the benefit of those who like a road map to a book's contents three reasons can be given for placing the contents of the first chapter at the beginning. First, and by far the most influential, is that in a large congregation the first year of a senior minister's tenure often is crucial. The pace of congregational life is faster in big churches than in small ones, the turnover rate is higher, and the leadership role of the pastor is more central. By contrast, in most small congregations, where continuity is the theme, the foundation for change may not be laid until the second or third year of a new pastorate. In most large churches, however, where discontinuity usually is a fact of life, it often is essential for the new senior minister to accept that leadership role during the crucial first year.

A second reason for placing that chapter first is, with but three exceptions, most senior ministers share that common experience of a first year as the new senior minister. One exception, of course, is the pastor who organizes a new congregation and stays as that congregation grows in numbers to the point that the founding pastor becomes the senior minister of what is now a multiple-staff church. The second is the person who comes on the scene as an associate minister and subsequently replaces the departed senior pastor. The third, and most common exception, is the pastor who comes to a small or middle-sized congregation, helps it see and realize its potential for growth and eventually becomes the senior minister of a large multiple-staff church without moving.

The third reason for this sequence is the skeleton for the outline is the ministerial journey of that composite couple, the Reverend Mr. and Mrs. Donald Johnson and this book begins with their first year at First Church. Those interested in the earlier years and pilgrimage of this couple may want to turn to *The Pastor and the People,* rev. ed. (Nashville: Abingdon Press, 1986), which describes their ministry at a composite parish named St. John's Church.

The reason the second chapter is placed next and the reason it is so long is that building and nurturing a staff is a high priority for most senior ministers. That also often turns out to be one of the most urgent and complex responsibilities of the newly arrived senior minister.

The third chapter comes this early partly to lift up the importance of music in the large church and partly because this also is a delicate issue. Many newly arrived senior ministers need to look at alternatives for staffing the ministry of music before building a program staff and seven of those alternatives are described in this third chapter.

While real estate and financial concerns really are

means-to-an-end issues and ideally could be relegated to an appendix, in real life the newly arrived senior minister often finds (a) one or both have been neglected and need urgent attention, (b) if neglected, one or both may become barriers to focusing on ministry, (c) the state of one or both often influences congregational self-esteem, (d) one or both may be an opportunty to produce some early victories, and (e) these victories can help shift the congregational orientation from nostalgic discussions about the past to optimistic hopes for the future. In addition, limitations of real estate or financial resources frequently can be huge barriers to evangelism and numerical growth.

The fifth chapter begins with some reflections on staff relationships and the future of the number-one associate minister and eventually moves on to two of the most troublesome issues facing many senior ministers. One is the revitalization of the women's organization to enable it to reach a generation of younger women and the second is the expansion of the adult Sunday school. At this point an apology to the reader is due. In a book of this scope it is impossible to offer suggestions on all areas of ministry such as community outreach, evangelism, missions, social concerns, day care for either children or mature adults, aerobic dance classes, and dozens of other programs that do concern many senior ministers.

One reason for placing such a heavy emphasis on these two organizations is the new senior minister often is expected to lead in their revitalization. A second is that in many congregations these two organizations constitute the heart of the organized group life of that church.

For many senior ministers the sixth chapter is the one that gets to the heart of reality. For most senior ministers life is centered around Sunday morning. This chapter offers suggestions on several aspects of that part of the week.

Those who have read through the book before returning to this introduction will have already discovered that the seventh chapter discusses a variety of subjects which did not fit comfortably or conveniently into earlier chapters. Some readers may find this to be the most interesting chapter of all since it is concerned with frustrations and questions repeatedly raised by hundreds of senior ministers.

Finally, three other introductory comments need to be made. For those who wonder how this volume relates to the earlier book, *The Multiple Staff and the Larger Church* (Nashville: Abingdon Press, 1980), the answer comes in three parts. First, that book focused primarily on the distinctive nature of the large church. This one has been written to, for, and about senior ministers. Also, this one is based on eight additional years of working with large churches and with senior ministers. Perhaps most important of all, this book places a greater emphasis on the role of the senior minister and of other staff members and less on a congregation-wide perspective.

Second, for those who may be concerned about the data base, this book is based largely on twenty-seven years of parish consultations with churches of all sizes from three dozen denominations. Many of these congregations averaged between 300 and 5,000 at worship on Sunday morning. The second basic source has been conversations with approximately a thousand senior ministers from over four dozen denominations in seminars, workshops, parish consultations, and individual interviews. This has been accompanied by conversations with approximately 1,700 associate ministers, 800 lay program associates, and literally thousands of other lay staff members and leaders, both volunteer and paid. The third source is extensive reading in the literature, some of which is cited here and some is cited in earlier books.

The last of these introductory comments is directed at those who worry about separating fact from fiction. The decision to use a composite couple, Don and Mary Johnson, was chosen as a means of illustrating many of the issues and questions facing a senior minister. These are composite characters. Neither Don nor Mary represent any one person. Their experiences, however, including the surprise gift of a huge amount of money by a relatively inactive member, described in chapter 4, are taken from real life. All the experiences, much of the dialogue, and all of the programmatic and staff concepts are drawn from real life experiences this observer encountered in consultations with large congregations. It also should be noted most references to dollars are in terms of the 1988 value of the American dollar and may have to be adjusted for Canadian readers or for inflation.

The obvious implication of this last paragraph is that I am deeply indebted to thousands of people, both lay and clergy, who have been my instructors over the past twenty-seven years in the life, ministry, outreach, mysteries, and culture of the large Protestant church. They also have helped me understand at least a little about that unique vocation of serving as a senior minister, the expectations and demands placed on those who accept that call and the complexities of life in that role. It is impossible to name them all, but I am grateful!

In addition, by their witness and their words these people have helped me sustain my confidence in the worshiping community as God's instrument here on earth. The local church is not only a place where the word is preached and the sacraments are celebrated, but it also is a place for pilgrims to come for inspiration, guidance, challenge, renewal, and the opportunity to serve. For that I also am thankful.

That Critical First Year

Chapter One

"Well, it looks as if we're about to begin a new era here at First Church," observed Pat Andrews as they stopped at Terry Brown's house for a cup of coffee after the first trustees' meeting following Don Johnson's arrival as the new senior minister.

"I'm not sure I know what you mean," responded Terry, "but if you're referring to Pastor Johnson's willingness to confront the issues head on, I say it's about time!"

"That's exactly what I mean," replied Pat. "He came in with his laundry list of what needed to be done and, as nearly as I can figure it out, he gave us trustees a choice of getting things done or he would look elsewhere for help."

"That's not exactly what he said," objected Terry. "I'm nearing the end of my second term as a trustee, and I can remember that at my first meeting five years ago, we talked about the need to remodel the fellowship hall, but nothing had ever been said about buying that little store on the corner before tonight. Dr. Bennington, who had been here as the senior minister for at least six or seven years at the time, made it clear that while he was not satisfied with the condition of the fellowship hall, he wasn't going to push it. He told us clearly that it was up to the members in general and the trustees in particular to do something about it. He told us he could live with it if we were all satisfied with it."

"Yeah, I remember that," recalled Pat. "I was on the

finance committee at the time and a couple of the trustees came to us and asked for about a quarter of a million dollars for the remodeling, and we told them that was not at the top of our priority list and, as far as I can recall, that was the end of that until tonight."

"My hunch is that renovation of the fellowship hall not only is back on the agenda," suggested Terry, "but that it will be under way before another year rolls around. This guy strikes me as someone who gets things done."

Six weeks earlier the Reverend Mr. Don Johnson had arrived as the new senior minister of the 103-year-old First Church. He was following the twelve-year pastorate of Edward Bennington who was planning to remain in the community for at least the first five years of his retirement. Mrs. Bennington, now sixty-one years old, needed four more years of service as a teacher in the public school system before she could receive a full pension. Dr. Bennington had been looking forward to retirement for at least three or four years and his tenure officially had come to an end on June 30.

A special committee had arranged a big farewell dinner for Dr. and Mrs. Bennington a few days before his departure and presented him with a check for slightly over $5,000 as a farewell gift. The farewell dinner had been held at a new hotel out near the interchange on the interstate highway. The committee chose that location for several reasons. They wanted it to be a high class event, they expected at least 600 or 700 people to attend, and the sixty-eight-year-old fellowship hall would seat only 400. Actually only 385 people came, in part because the cost was $45 per couple. When this farewell dinner was first proposed, the leaders in the women's fellowship had made it very clear they had zero interest in preparing a meal for that size crowd in what they say was a small and obsolete kitchen or in serving a meal in late June in a building that was not air-conditioned.

Three days after his last Sunday in the pulpit at First Church, Dr. and Mrs. Bennington had left for a six-week tour of Europe and the Holy Land, so they were out-of-town when Don and Mary arrived.

Dr. Bennington had announced his retirement the previous September and by the following February Don had been selected as Bennington's successor.[1] In late April, Mary and Don had come to town and made an offer to purchase a home which was accepted after an exchange of counter offers. They moved the last week in June, and Don was in the pulpit at First Church on the first Sunday in July. Since he came from another state, Don had only a superficial acquaintance with Dr. Bennington, but he had become fairly well acquainted with First Church's history, role, resources, problems, and, from Don's perspective, its potentialities.

This was the fourth pastorate for the forty-eight-year-old Don Johnson, and he came from eleven years as the pastor of St. John's Church, which had grown in size from an average attendance at worship of 199 the year before Don arrived to 328 in his last full year. One reason the committee wanted Don was his record at St. John's where the numerical decline of the previous six years had been reversed and followed by more than a 50 percent increase in attendance.

One reason Don was attracted to First Church was that he was convinced it still had great potential for ministry and outreach.

While the records are not of the best quality for the pre-1950 era, Don was told that in 1925 First Church had been averaging nearly 700 in Sunday school and over 500 in worship. The next quarter century saw a gradual decline in membership and attendance, an even sharper decline in financial support and an aging of the membership.

The new minister who arrived on September 1, 1950, reported that for 1950 worship attendance had averaged 185 and the Sunday school was down to an average of 140. When he left in 1964, worship attendance had been averaging between 600 and 700 for five consecutive years and the Sunday school had peaked in 1961 with an average attendance of 485.

His departure was followed by (1) the turbulent 1960s, (2) a thirty-eight-year-old senior minister with a deep concern for issue-centered ministries who displayed little interest in people and was able to attribute the sharp decline in worship attendance and the steep drop in Sunday school attendance as normal and acceptable developments for a downtown church of that era, (3) a fire in 1967 that destroyed part of the historic gothic sanctuary, provided a powerful rallying point for a group of lay volunteer and resulted in a $1.3 million rebuilding of the sanctuary, offices, rest rooms, parlor, and two classrooms, (4) a new senior minister who was forty-nine years old when he arrived in 1969 and fifty-five when he ran off with a member of the choir twenty years his junior in 1975, (5) an extended period with a fatherly intentional interim minister who helped the remaining members restore their respect for the office of pastor, and (6) the twelve-year pastorate of Edward Bennington who had an earned reputation as an excellent preacher, enjoyed calling, especially on prospective new members, but was a "let's not rock the boat" non-directive leader.

Between 1976 and Bennington's departure the average attendance at worship had climbed back up from 165 to 350, thanks largely to the senior minister's preaching and calling, the financial situation had been stabilized, the mortgage from the reconstruction following the fire was paid off, and the program staff had been expanded to include a senior pastor, an associate minister, a part-time director of Christian education, and a full-time youth minister. The first person to fill this recently created position of youth minister was Anne Potter, a twenty-seven-year-old minister who had had the highest academic grade point of anyone in her seminary graduating class and also had won the preaching prize in her senior year.

The thirty-three-year-old associate minister, who had wanted to succeed Dr. Bennington, had left in anger and frustration two months before Don's arrival. Anne, who was convinced the associate minister was incompetent, lazy, and ignorant, in addition to being an outstanding example of a male chauvinist pig, was delighted when she heard that he was departing.

The staff also included a fifty-nine-year-old ex-farmer and his wife, Virgil and Nellie Meyer, who had moved to the city four years earlier when their son-in-law and daughter had taken over the family farm where Virgil had lived all his life. They served as the custodians of the building and lived in a small apartment over the fellowship hall. For the next eight years Don bragged that First Church had the best custodial staff of any congregation in the western hemisphere. Virgil Meyer had spent forty-five years learning how to take the initiative, how to plan ahead, how to be a productive worker, and how to fix anything that was broken. Mrs. Meyer conveyed the impression that cleanliness came even before godliness. They adopted First Church to replace the loss in their life of the family farm which their daughter and son-in-law had purchased. Several leaders contended that Dr. Bennington's number-one contribution to First Church was finding this couple.

The office staff included a full-time clerk-typist-receptionist, Sarah Larkin, who carried the title of church secretary and a full-time pastor's secretary, who a year earlier had announced she was leaving when her husband retired the following May. At Dr. Bennington's suggestion, that position had been filled on an interim basis so Don could choose a permanent successor. A couple of months after his arrival, Don had found his new secretary, a fifty-three-year-old woman, Lillian Dempsey, who was married to the pastor of a Conservative Baptist congregation on the north side of town. She had been reared in the Methodist Church, mothered three children, had worked as a secretary previously in three other churches, understood her number-one loyalty was to Don, not to First Church, and was never surprised when someone behaved in a manner that was not fully Christian. She soon became Don's alter ego, the hub of the internal communication network and the keeper of the church calendar.

Choices for That First Year

Even before entering seminary Don had heard the conventional wisdom that advises the newly arrived minister not to rock the boat during the first year, to learn the lay of the land, to get acquainted with the people, and to be slow and cautious in introducing new ideas or making changes.

Don had followed that advice in his first two pastorates. In the first one it had fit the circumstances. There was no boat to rock, and all the people wanted, expected, or permitted was for the minister to bury the dead, baptize the children, comfort the ill, preach the gospel, meet with the youth, work with the Sunday school, and love everyone.

When he first arrived in his third pastorate, Don was still convinced his role was to be an enabler, but the circumstances at St. John's forced him to rethink that concept. St. John's needed an initiating leader. Don changed his whole approach to ministerial leadership while at St. John's, enjoyed it, saw the church prosper, felt the people respond in a positive and creative fashion, and left convinced that as the size of the congregation increased, so did the expectations of the members in regard to the pastor's willingness to accept the role as an initiating leader.[2]

When the forty-eight-year-old Don Johnson arrived at First Church, after twenty-three years as a minister, he was somewhere between prepared and eager to accept his leadership role. As it turned out, he did not have any other choice. He found that Dr. Bennington had spent the last four years looking forward to retirement and the congregation resembled a textbook example of the passive church.[3] While the disharmony among the staff had been papered over by the fatherly Dr. Bennington by one resignation and one retirement, it was a fact that could not be ignored.

The last new adult class in the Sunday school had been organized eleven years earlier. The music program consisted of a twenty-voice chancel choir, a twelve-member youth handbell choir, and two children's choirs. The number of circles in the women's fellowship had shrunk from nine to six, despite an increase in the total membership of the congregation.

While Don's compensation including cash salary and housing was exactly the same as Dr. Bennington had been receiving, this represented a $2,400 reduction from his compensation at St. John's Church and that fact disturbed several leaders.

Don was tremendously impressed with the gifts, skills, personality, enthusiasm, and commitment of Anne Potter, who was completing her second year on the staff. Don was convinced Anne was overqualified for her position and underutilized. A month after he arrived, he asked her, "Anne, what do you see you do best as a minister?"

"Preach, teach, and plan new programs," replied Anne with no hesitation.

"That's interesting," replied Don. "My recollection is you told me last week you had preached only on seven Sundays since your arrival two years ago, and I understand your primary responsibility is youth ministries. If I heard you correctly, you did not include that in the list of what you do best. What are you doing here? Why aren't you serving as a pastor of a church where you can preach every Sunday and do what you say you do best?"

"Because I'm a woman and it's still hard for a young single woman fresh out of seminary to get the church of her choice," replied Anne. "The trade-off was to be in a big church in a place where I wanted to live even though it means my primary responsibility is not my number-one competence or preference. If you were a woman, you would understand life is full of trade-offs."

"I think I understand that, but maybe not as clearly as you do," admitted Don. "How long do you expect to be here at First Church?"

"That depends," declared Anne. "That depends on your expectations of me and it depends on what kind of opportunities I'm offered to go out and be the pastor of my own church."

"Let's make a deal," offered Don. "If you'll promise me you'll stay at least one more year, I'll try to make your ministry here a little more rewarding, and I'll do everything I can to help you find a church where you can utilize all your gifts. Frankly, I don't think you're cut out to be a career associate, and that's what we need here."

"That's a deal," agreed Anne, "if you promise me I can preach ten Sundays a year."

"That's fair," replied Don, "and let's identify those ten Sundays as soon as we can."

One afternoon several days after his arrival Don asked Virgil and Nellie Meyer, the custodians, to introduce him to the building. As they walked into fellowship hall, Virgil said,

"While I've never seen any, I'm reasonably sure we have rats here."

"That's ridiculous," snapped Don. "You can't have rats in a downtown church building!"

"I agree we shouldn't," answered Virgil, "but I've seen enough rats in my life to be pretty sure we have rats here."

"What should we do?" asked Don.

"Well, I've tried to poison them," explained Virgil, "but they're pretty smart and I don't think it's worked. What we really should do is completely remodel this entire wing. That means tearing out all the insides of all three floors, building a new kitchen, new floors, a new electrical system and also remodeling the rest rooms here on this floor as well as the classrooms on the second and third floors. The other half of the building is in good shape; that was completely remodeled after the fire in 1967."

"What else do we need?" asked Don.

"I thought you might ask that," replied Virgil as he pulled a list out of his pocket. "If we remodel this wing, we also should install a new boiler, air-condition at least the kitchen and fellowship hall, put in an elevator, and remodel the entrance into this wing so it's more attractive from the outside since about half of our people come in this way on Sunday morning. There also is a small store next door that has twelve off-street parking spaces. I know the owner who runs the store, and he is getting ready to put it on the market. If we bought it and tore down the store, we could add about thirty off-street parking spaces. As you probably noticed, we only have forty parking spaces that we own, but there are three large parking lots within a block, one owned by a bank, one by a savings and loan association, and one by the city. There's enough parking around here for Sunday morning, but we are short for daytime activities and on some evenings."

"What would it cost to buy that store and lot?" inquired Don.

"My guess is $300,000, maybe less," replied Virgil, "but if we don't buy it soon, someone else will and we may not have another chance for a long time."

"What about your apartment upstairs?" asked Don, who had not seen it. "What does it need?"

"It's O.K.," replied Nellie. "It was completely remodeled before we moved in and it doesn't need a thing. We keep it in good shape."

Where Does the Time Go?

Like many newly arrived senior ministers following a long pastorate, Don Johnson spent most of his time during those first few months on a dozen responsibilities.

1. Seekng to identify and to understand the distinctive characteristics and the subculture of this congregation. As a part of that effort Pastor Johnson was deeply interested in identifying the vision or myth or energizing force that both held this large collection of people together and also motivated them to be a part of *this* worshiping community. The oral tradition at First Church soon revealed to Don that decades earlier the energizing force had been the Reverend James T. Doyle who had carved out an influential place in the city during his fourteen-year pastorate from 1950 to 1964.

The next powerful unifying force apparently was the fire of 1967 and the decision to rebuild downtown, rather than to relocate. More recently the fatherly personality of Dr. Bennington stood out.

What else held this place together, wondered Don, and what made it function? Obviously part of the answer to that question included habit, friendship ties of the members with one another, shared memories, inertia, the attachment to this sacred place, and institutional loyalties, but a vision that both energized and unified appeared to be absent.

2. Meeting people and learning names, roles, and relationships.

3. Making sure that every Sunday morning offered the people a carefully planned and fast paced worship experience with an excellent sermon.

4. Getting acquainted with the staff and beginning the process of conceptualizing what his ideal staff would look like three years hence. In this case the most urgent task was to replace the pastor's secretary who had left a few months earlier, and Lillian Dempsey came in to fill that vacancy.

5. Attempting to comprehend the total program and ministry of this congregation and identifying (a) the strengths and (b) the gaps, inconsistencies, and holes.

6. Making a special effort to get acquainted with all the fringe members and those who had lapsed into inactivity on the premise that the arrival of a new minister is perceived by many fringe and inactive members as the most attractive reentry point back into a more active role. Don recognized from past experience that if he did not do this during those first six months, he never again would have the time, and they probably would never again be as receptive.

7. Calling on former leaders to build relationships with them, benefit from their experience and wisdom, gain an understanding of their perspective, and earn their confidence.

8. Studying the system for the enlistment and assimilation of new members. As Don called on several dozen persons who had joined during the past few years, he learned (a) the heart of that "system" really was the warm and attractive personality of Dr. Bennington who had devoted considerable time to calling on prospective new members and (b) that system had left town about the same week Don arrived.

9. Identifying and building relationships with the four to five dozen people who were the core of the lay volunteer network for doing ministry at First Church and who also carried much of the administrative load. Don was slightly surprised to learn that four of the most valuable volunteers technically were not members, but they saw this as an insignificant fact.

Concurrently with this effort Don spent a fair amount of time attempting to identify potential new allies for the days and months ahead.

10. Learning about all the special concerns of First Church in the field of community outreach and missions. Don was surprised and delighted as he learned the variety and extent of this dimension of First Church's ministry.

It also became clear to Don that Dr. Bennington's three major interests had been preaching, calling on prospective new members, and missions. That also helped explain why several other areas of congregational life had been neglected.

11. Spending at least a modest amount of time becoming acquainted with other members of the clergy in what was clearly a different religious subculture from the last community in which he had served.

12. Building a list of what needed attention. One reason for building this list was the obviously large number of concerns that had been neglected in recent years. As one of Don's new friends at First Church subsequently confided to him, "During his last few years Dr. Bennington moved into what might be called a pre-retirement stance and the congregation joined him." Much needed to be done, and Don believed the way to do this was to do it. In addition, this would be a means of overcoming the passivity that filled the atmosphere at First Church. Most important of all, however, was the need to do what needed to be done to enable First Church to be free to fulfill its potential in ministry and outreach. Finally, Don, by his style and personality was a list-builder, so he built a list.

Building That List

Within a couple of weeks following his arrival Don had identified a long list of items that needed attention and had begun to identify the people who might help transform some of these needs into reality.

At the top of the list was the need to find someone to replace the departed pastor's secretary. The temporary replacement had made it very clear to Don on his first day in the office that her commitment to fill in for a few months expired on August 31 at the latest. She was a loyal and committed member of First Church, but she had explained to Don, "My husband did not approve my taking this job. In the first place he is thoroughly convinced that a church should never put a member on the payroll. In the second place he took early retirement in May, and we're leaving on a cruise the second week in September. I'll stay until August 31, but I hope you can find someone sooner." A week before the deadline, Lillian Dempsey, the wife of the Baptist minister, began work and so that issue no longer was on Don's list.

1. Acquiring the store and parking lot on the corner as

soon as the owner decided to place it on the market. (The three most widely heard cries of frustration from leaders of urban churches are (a) "We used to own it and we sold it," (b) "We could have bought it for a song, but now it would cost a fortune," and (c) "We had a chance to buy it, we turned it down and now when we need it, that property simply is not available at any price.") After hearing Virgil's explanation of its possible availability, Don placed this near the top of the list.

2. Creating a system for the enlistment of new members. The records indicated that for the past five years First Church had been losing an average of fourteen members by death every year, another thirty by transfer and an average of a half dozen by action of the governing board as they removed the names of inactive members. Don was reasonably sure that First Church also was experiencing the loss of at least three or four dozen members a year of people who simply "dropped out." They disappeared without asking for a letter of transfer. This was an eight-hundred-member congregation and the dropout rate in churches of that size rarely is lower than 4 percent annually and frequently exceeds 7 to 10 percent. The relatively low ratio of worship attendance-to-membership indicated the membership roll included many people who no longer identified themselves with First Church. Don was convinced that First Church had to receive an average of at least seventy-five new members annually simply to remain on a plateau in size and probably would need to add a hundred or more new members every year in order to experience any significant numerical growth.

3. Planning a big celebration on the fifth anniversary of the arrival of Mr. and Mrs. Meyer as resident custodians. Don had sounded out several longtime members on this, and it was clear this would be an event that would produce many eager co-conspirators. The date for next February soon was secretly set by Don and three former leaders who enthusiastically agreed these two loyal and faithful friends deserved some highly visible recognition.

4. Redefining and expanding the role of Anne Potter's position. Within a week after their arrival, Don told his wife,

Mary, "While I think she'll be moving on before too long, Anne is a tremendously talented minister who is overqualified and underutilized here. If we expand her responsibilities, she may be willing to stay a little longer."

5. Expanding the ministry of music and taking advantage of the power of music in a big congregation.

In several respects Don felt this was both the most urgent and the most complex item on this list. The part-time choir director, John Owen, owned and operated his own music store. He was a reasonably competent, but uninspiring and unimaginative choir director who had built a strong support group from among eight or ten members of the choir. He had joined First Church in 1958, back when he was a young clerk in the music store he now owned. When the choir director of thirty years tenure had retired in 1962, John had been hired as her replacement. He had initiated the bequest that had enabled First Church to purchase a full set of handbells, and he also directed the high school handbell choir. Four volunteers organized, rehearsed, and directed the two children's choirs, one with twelve third and fourth graders and the other with ten fifth and sixth graders.

That was the music program at First Church. It was clear to Pastor Johnson that the potential was there for a thirty-five- to forty-voice chancel choir, but a new director would be required to attract that many volunteers, and if John Owen were forced out, perhaps a dozen members of the present choir might quit in protest.

6. Revitalizing the women's organization was an obvious need, but cowardly Don placed that on his list of concerns that could wait another year or two.

7. Rebuilding the Sunday school was a need that at least sixty members had informed Pastor Johnson should be at or near the top of the priority list. Nearly one-third of the most active leaders in the Sunday school informed him that could not happen without replacing the present director of Christian education, about a fourth explained to Don that she was irreplaceable, and the rest of the teachers and leaders decided they would let the new senior minister figure that one out without their advice.

8. Replacing the recently departed associate minister was high on the priority list for many members, but Don was sure that could and should wait until after several other decisions had been made.

About two weeks after his arrival Don, in separate one-to-one conversations, had asked Anne Potter and a half dozen volunteers, "Would you tell me just exactly what that associate minister did here? He left two months before I arrived, and I've never met the guy. Just what did he do?"

The best answer came from Anne. "Wait and ask me that same question six weeks from now."

Six weeks later Don asked Anne, "Well, the six weeks are up. What did he do?"

Anne replied, "What do you think he did?"

"As far as I can tell, he didn't do much of anything except sit in on several meetings and preach a half dozen times a year."

"You're right," declared Anne. "That's why you are so lucky. You've got a vacant position to fill, no hurry to fill it, and I'll be glad to do the preaching he did. When you add everything up, you've got a $42,000 compensation package to work with as you build your own staff, but no extra work to do because of the vacancy."

Just to be sure, Don checked with Virgil on the former associate minister's responsibilities. After hearing what Don had learned, honest Virgil said, "That's not quite right. He also spent a lot of time reading, and he taught a women's Bible class every October for four Tuesday afternoons, but last October only three or four women showed up for the class."

Several years later one of the members, who was a personnel specialist, gave Don a different perspective on that situation as he explained, "One of the differences between you and Dr. Bennington is you know how to utilize staff. Several years ago we got this new associate minister straight out of seminary. He came with impressive recommendations from several professors, but he knew very little about the church. He had grown up in a small rural church in Pennsylvania, been a part of a small campus group while attending the university and worshiped with the seminary community before coming here. He had spent his intern year with a two-church parish in Nebraska. When he came here, he found we already had a part-time youth director, he did not know how to plan and implement new programs, the DCE bossed him around like he was her errand boy, Dr. Bennington apparently concluded that since he had been to seminary, he knew how to do ministry. The fact of the matter was, he needed a lot of supervision and instruction, and he just didn't get it. He had not learned how to work, how to initiate, how to enlist a team of volunteers, or how to build program, so he spent a lot of time in his study reading and he sat in on meetings. My hunch is he must have spent at least two hundred hours preparing for each sermon he preached. Anne Potter did not help the situation any after she arrived. She's a classic overachiever and really a self-starter. As she compared her salary with his and her productivity with his, she couldn't help but feel he was either lazy or incompetent. I think we really did that young man a serious disservice by not creating a supportive work environment for him where he could have learned how to be an effective and productive pastor."

"I had a hunch that might have been part of the story," reflected Don, "but you're the first one to explain to me what really happened."

"By contrast," continued the personnel specialist, "it is clear you know how to help all the staff members set goals, manage their time, derive satisfactions from their work, and see themselves as a part of a team working on a larger task."

"I try," replied Don modestly, "but the Lord has blessed us with some highly talented staff members."

"Hogwash!" retorted his friend. "The Lord blesses those who help themselves and you've built a crackerjack staff and you know how to get the most out of their gifts, talents, experience, and time."

9. Renovating the fellowship hall was an obvious need, but how to finance it was a big puzzle. Virgil told Don one day that he had asked a couple of members who were contractors for a ball park estimate and they had agreed the cost would be well over half a million dollars for the renovation of that wing

built back in the 1920s and it might run as high as $750,000 or more.

10. Increasing the Sunday morning worship attendance was a goal that Don had set for himself even before his arrival. During his first interview he had been troubled by the fact that an 806-member congregation was averaging only 350 at Sunday morning worship. Don was convinced the attendance-to-membership ratio should be at least 60 percent and at First Church it was only 43 percent. He wasn't sure why that ratio was not higher. It could be the membership roll was inflated. It could be that many members attended only once or twice a month. It could be that a large number of members attended only a few times a year.

July and August obviously were not the best months to make an accurate diagnosis of the situation. Despite vacations and the normal summer slump, attendance averaged close to 340 during Don's first ten weeks at First Church, including the two Sundays when Anne preached. Don recognized that was due in part to the fact that the arrival of a new minister usually produces at least a temporary spurt in attendance. Pastor Johnson's first serious effort to deal with this issue came when he scheduled a survey of worship attendance for October, but more on that in chapter 6.

11. Scheduling a capital funds campaign was an obvious need that Don recognized during that first interview. The level of member giving was good. During Dr. Bennington's last full year as senior minister, member giving came to a total of $357,800, up from $339,000 the previous year. In addition, First Church received $28,000 annually from an endowment fund and approximately $20,000 in fees so the budget of $405,000 was fully underwritten.

There was, however, no trustees' fund for maintenance of the property or for capital improvements and the real estate clearly needed some attention. Ideally, Don dreamed, we could raise a million dollars in one appeal next spring to purchase the store on the corner, expand and resurface the parking area, and renovate the wing that included the fellowship hall. In his more realistic hours he concluded a goal of $500,000 might be more easily attained.

12. Envisioning a new dream or a new vision of a new role for First Church was the most perplexing item on this list. What is the Lord calling First Church to be and to do in the years just ahead of us? Don asked himself that question scores of times during that first year. At most of the three dozen home meetings he and Mary had attended during those first months to become acquainted with the members, Don had raised that question as a discussion starter. He had asked it at meetings of the governing board and various committees. On several occasions when he had gone to lunch with current leaders, he had used that question as a means of changing the agenda from the casual get-acquainted-with-the-new-minister conversation to eliciting creative responses. The most frequent responses included, "To be a vital church," "to be a redemptive community," "to be a beacon of faith and hope in this community," "to glorify God," "to save souls," "to proclaim the Good News," "to welcome newcomers to share in our journey of faith," "to preach Christ crucified," "to be a reconciling community in a divided world," "to be a place where parents can bring their children to learn about God," and "to win people to Christ."

After hearing these and other answers for several months, Don finally accepted as a fact that in a big congregation such as First Church, the vision must come from the leadership. After 103 years First Church had accumulated so many layers of generations of members that it represented a highly diverse collection of people with sharply differing views on almost every subject from nuclear deterrence to the central purpose of the church to euthanasia to how loudly the organ should be played to abortion on demand to the importance of the Sunday school to the proper attire for Sunday morning worship to how candidates for the presidency should be selected to the appropriate compensation for a senior minister to the value of a college degree.

Who Creates That Vision?

As he discovered this range of diversity, which was far greater than that he remembered as the pattern at St. John's Church, Don realized that if a new vision of a new tomorrow for First Church was to come out of the people and to be widely supported, that process would require between three and ten decades and hundreds of funerals.

Ten years later most of the members, as they looked back at what had happened since Don's arrival, lifted up specific events or activities that had occurred during the third or fourth years of Don's ministry as the critical turning points or as the influential forks in the road. One longtime leader categorically declared, "The new era began when we dedicated the remodeled fellowship hall. The size of the crowd that turned out that evening and the enthusiasm that was nearly universal was the turning point in the life of this congregation. That came during Pastor Johnson's third year and that set the stage for all that followed."

When she heard that interpretation of the past, another longtime leader at First Church retorted, "No, the remodeling of the fellowship hall was only a highly visible and unifying means-to-an-end. The beginning point of this new era in our history came during Pastor Johnson's sixth year when we averaged over 700 at Sunday morning worship and broke the old record that had been set more than thirty years earlier. That convinced everyone we were in a new era."

Don Johnson knew, however, that the crucial year was his first year at First Church, and everything that had followed had been built on the foundation laid during that first year. As a general rule, the larger the congregation, the more critical that first year of a new pastorate is in building the foundation for what follows. From a long-term congregational perspective the events and activities of the third or fourth or fifth or sixth year may stand out as watershed happenings, but the wise senior minister recognizes the value of building an action agenda during that crucial first year and of enlisting allies to help implement that agenda.

What Is Realistic?

After nearly a quarter of a century as a pastor, after reading dozens of books and articles on planned change, after watching the new principal of the high school in their former city go through a frustrating five years of trying to change that school and after reflecting on his own experiences, Don had come up with what he saw as a realistic set of expectations for that year.

First, he recognized the importance of accepting the role as *the professional* leader at First Church. He was the professionally trained person serving on a full-time basis whom the part-time lay volunteers looked to for direction, initiative, inspiration, and support. Don recognized First Church was too large to function effectively as a lay-led congregation. The pastor has to lead.

Second, he was convinced that during that crucial first year it is possible to help people become aware of new possibilities, to begin to grasp a new vision and to help them look down a new road, but there is a limit on how many changes can be accomplished during the first year.

Third, that first year could be very critical in beginning the process of changing the culture. That means setting up some new structures to support that new vision, of creating some new traditions that are consistent with that new vision, and of beginning to change some of the inherited values, customs, and habits.

Fourth, as was pointed out earlier, that first year is an excellent time to identify and enlist allies who will help turn that vision into reality.

Fifth, Don recognized and affirmed the power of symbols, rituals, celebration, and victories. When people asked why he wanted to celebrate the 104th anniversary of the founding of First Church, one of his responses was, "So we'll have more practice behind us when the time comes to celebrate the 105th anniversary."

A few months after his arrival, he had asked for a special committee to be appointed to design a logogram or symbol that could be used on the bulletin board in front of the building, on letterheads, calling cards, bulletin covers, and as a lapel pin. At that 104th anniversary celebration near the end of Don's first year, a special version of that pin was presented to every person who had been a member of First Church for fifty or more years. The following year a slightly different version was presented to those who had been members of First Church for a quarter century or longer.

The people who proudly wore those pins not only had allegiance to First Church reinforced, they also found it a little easier to forgive this brash new senior minister when he pushed for changes they felt were unnecessary or premature.

The fire of 1967 had destroyed several dozen framed photographs that filled the hallways. When he learned of this loss, which had been ignored for two decades, Don organized a special committee of longtime members to discover what could be done. A year later a wall in one corridor was lined with photographs of most of the ministers who had served this congregation during the previous hundred years.

Don also initiated a practice he had found to be a powerful force back at St. John's. By late October one wall in every room of the children's division of the Sunday school was covered with individual pictures of each member of that class. When a first-time visitor appeared, a child was sent to bring the official Sunday school photographer—a thirteen-year-old boy who could not tolerate the immaturity of junior high school youth and spent every Sunday as the volunteer staff person in the audio-visual room. Before the class was over that day, the first-time visitor was urged, "Be sure to come back next Sunday morning and see your picture up on the wall with the rest of our class."

At the end of the Sunday school year the pictures from each class were collected and mounted in an attractive frame with the name below each picture. These were hung in the corridor and reinforced each child's sense of belonging.

Another facet of Don's determination to utilize the power of photographs had to be postponed for a few years. The large "gathering room" that was constructed later as a combination entrance into the sanctuary from the parking lot, addition to the fellowship hall, and social center following worship had one large blank wall. On this wall were mounted, in order of seniority, photographs of all members on the day that room was first placed into use. That approach meant no one's picture had to be removed when they died or moved away or joined another church, and the pictures of new members could be added in order of seniority, rather than alphabetically. It also was an affirmation of tenure and made it easier for longtime members to locate and study the photographs of new members.

As part of a larger strategy to increase that ratio of church attendance to membership Pastor Johnson gradually began to schedule an increasing number of special Sundays.[4]

The most delicate issue the new senior minister faced in that crucial first year, however, was building a new staff.

Rebuilding the Staff

Chapter Two

Like most newly arrived senior ministers Don Johnson saw himself faced with a two-part strategy in regard to the staffing of First Church. The short-term strategy was responding to the situation where he was the new kid on the block and had to deal with the staff he had inherited. He recognized he was unusually fortunate in that he had inherited two vacancies plus at least three remarkably valuable players on the staff team.

At the top of the list of inherited valuable players were Virgil and Nellie Meyer. These two faithful servants of God not only had inherited the gift of enjoying hard work from their German ancestors, they also were committed Christians who truly loved the church. For more than three decades following their marriage they had been loyal and heavily involved members of a thrifty small rural congregation where Nellie had taught in the Sunday school, been president of the women's organization on at least a half dozen occasions, and also chaired the mission committee in her last five years there. Virgil had sung in the choir, chaired the finance committee, served as a trustee for over twenty years, worked with the high school youth group, and taught the only adult class in the Sunday school. The farm, the church, and the children had consumed well over 98 percent of their life for nearly four decades.

After four years on the staff, they were still shocked at how extravagant this big city church was in spending money, but they were determined they would neither contribute to that disease nor catch it. Some of the members joked that Virgil spent an hour every day all winter long going around turning out lights and turning the thermostats down a few degrees, but everyone appreciated their value system and admired their dedication.

A third valuable player was the miscast, overqualified, and underutilized Anne Potter. A few months after that conversation in which Anne had agreed to stay for at least one more year, Don dropped by Anne's office and asked, "Interested in renegotiating the contract?"

"That depends, what do you have in mind?" replied Anne.

"Well, as I told you before, I don't think you're cut out to be a career associate and you agreed with me, but I need to buy some time. If you agree to stay another two years, I would like to recommend that you be asked to fill the current vacancy we have for an associate pastor. You really don't want to do youth work, and we need to fill that vacancy for an associate minister so we can work out the rest of the staff configuration."

"That means I would stay until I'm about thirty," reflected Anne who had just celebrated her twenty-eighth birthday. "I guess I could agree to that if the people here want a woman as their associate pastor. Who'll work with youth?"

"Don't worry about that," replied Don. "Let's talk about what you will do. I want you to help me expand the program, preach ten or twelve Sundays a year, teach an adult class during the Sunday school hour and one during the week, do half of the calling including hospital visitation, and work with three or four standing committees."

"That's a lot better job than I have now," declared Anne without any hestitation. "I'll take it."

"It may take a month or two before this becomes official," warned Don, "but let's assume it will work out."

After that happy first step in building a new program staff, Don decided the time had come to tackle the more difficult ones. He made an appointment to go to her office and talk with the part-time director of Christian education about her future. During the intervening five days as Don openly fretted about this at home, Mary, his wife, asked, "It's pretty clear you want her to resign. How are you going to persuade her to leave quietly?"

"I don't know," replied Don. "That's why I asked her to set aside two hours on Thursday afternoon so we could talk without interruption."

"Why not simply lay out in detail what you have in mind for a new staff and ask her how she sees herself fitting into that picture?" suggested Mary.

The following Thursday afternoon Don walked into the office of the director of Christian education and after a few minutes of small talk began, "Neva, I would like to discuss with you what I have in mind for a staff team here at First Church and talk with you about how you might fit into that team."

Before he could get to the second paragraph of his rehearsed comments, Neva interrupted, "I was pretty sure that's what you wanted to talk about when you asked me to set aside two hours for you to come to see me in my office. I figured if you wanted to talk about the Christian education program here, you would have asked me to come to your office. When you said you wanted to talk with me in my office, I decided you wanted to talk about me. During the last three or four days I've prayed about it as I asked God to give me direction. Let me make it easy for you. I'm resigning. I don't think the people here really want a good Christian education program, I don't believe you want me to continue on the staff, and I really do believe a new senior minister has the right to build a new staff. What date do you want me to use as the date of my resignation?"

"That's a big load to dump on me all at once," protested Don in what was clearly a defensive tone of voice. "What made you think I wanted you to resign? What did I say that led you to that conclusion?"

"You didn't say anything directly," replied Neva, obviously eager to complete this whole unpleasant conversation. "It's what you didn't say and didn't do. You've never talked to me directly about what I see needs to be done here or about how long I expected to be on the staff. I may be part-time, but I'm not dumb. I can figure out what's going on and I realize I don't fit into your plans."

Without realizing that he had been doing it, Don Johnson had been utilizing one of the most widely followed methods of terminating employment of a staff member. This is the sending of nonverbal signals that cause the staff member to feel excluded. It is not the best system, but sometimes it is effective. In a few cases signals that never were sent are received by an overly sensitive person who quietly seeks another job. More often the signals are sent, sometimes deliberately, sometimes unintentionally, but not received.

While this experience made Don feel uncomfortable during the following few weeks whenever he encountered Neva face-to-face, he did learn three lessons. One lesson was to seek to be more direct with all staff members. A second was that he had been delivering signals he had not intended to send. A third lesson was that he exercised less direct control than he had assumed to be the case and much of his influence was indirect.

The most difficult decision Don faced as he set out to build a new staff concerned the future of Sarah Larkin, the sixty-one-year-old church secretary. Thirty-eight years earlier Sarah and her husband, Hank, had joined First Church as newlyweds. Twelve years later, when the youngest of her three children was in second grade, Sarah had been hired as a half-time typist. Five years later, when the church secretary resigned, Sarah had applied and been hired to become the full-time secretary of First Church. According to the oral tradition Sarah not only ran the office, she also ran the church. Many people told Don their impression was Sarah was in charge and Dr. Bennington worked for her. While they apparently had a harmonious relationship, that was largely a product of Dr. Bennington's ability to get along with anyone and everyone. It was clear to Don and to everyone else that after a quarter of a century on the job Sarah also represented the institutional memory of First Church. While she had not applied for the position, Sarah clearly was offended when Don asked Lillian Dempsey to be his secretary.

Sarah was perceived as a saint by scores of old-timers, as a "walking file cabinet" by those who needed information and as a tyrant by those she did not like. She kept all the membership and financial records and spent many hours weekly entering information, in what later were discovered to be a set of redundant ledgers filled with handwritten records. On at least a hundred days a year she either came in at seven in the morning or did not leave until six in the evening. When people telephoned the church office, if they were friends of Sarah, they almost invariably received a warm and friendly greeting. If the caller was not on that friendship list, however, the chances were at least 50-50 that Sarah's response would be hostile. Among her favorite adversaries were (a) outside groups that sought to use the facilities at First Church, (b) women who dared to seek ordination, and (c) people who did not take her advice. From day one Sarah had succeeded in placing Anne Potter on the defensive and one result was Anne did about 80 percent of her own secretarial work and found volunteers to do most of the rest.

Every man on both the trustees and the finance committees found Sarah to be a cooperative, warm, friendly, and pleasant person to work with, and they dismissed all complaints as without foundation. Five years earlier, Sarah had asked for an extra week of vacation instead of a salary increase and had repeated that request every subsequent year. One result was many who looked only at the budget and saw her working late on so many evenings and on Saturdays were convinced she was grossly underpaid. A second result was she often took a week's vacation with practically no advance notice and that greatly disrupted the routine for the rest of the staff.

Within a few weeks after his arrival Don Johnson came to two conclusions, (1) he had inherited a severe problem that should have been resolved by his predecessor before his retirement, and (2) he was not going to go out on a limb and tackle that one all by himself.

In the October following his arrival Don called together three younger members, two of whom were second or third generation members at First Church and all of whom were highly skilled in working with computers.

"One of the things we must do here is change to electronic data processing of both membership and financial records and also replace the office typewriters with word processors," explained Don as he met with the three in his office. "That is not my field of expertise and I don't intend to become an expert. You three are, and I would like you three to study this and recommend the kind of installation we need. I've talked with both the trustees and the board, and they agree the time has come to make the change."

Two months later a detailed plan of action was presented to the board and Don suggested a special five-person action committee be appointed to implement the plan. Two of the five came from the study committee, one was a trustee, one came from the finance committee, and one was a fifty-five-year-old woman who was widely respected and a longtime acquaintance of Sarah's.

In addition to purchasing the recommended equipment and software, this ad hoc committee arranged a two-week training program for Don's secretary, Lillian Dempsey, to learn a new skill. When the committee sat down with Sarah to discuss her role in the system, she insisted the ledgers must be maintained in case the equipment broke down or someone needed information and did not know how to get it out of the computer. She proposed a new position of computer programmer be added to the office staff and she would be allowed to continue as the church secretary until she retired.

Two of the members of the committee insisted that one of the reasons for the change was to be able to secure more information more easily. Another reason was to reduce the work load, not to increase the office staff. After two more meetings Sarah decided to shift to a confrontational approach. "If you try to force me to learn to use this equipment, I'll resign!"

The widely respected fifty-five-year-old woman who chaired this ad hoc action committee said, "Sarah, I think I'm old enough to know how you feel, and if you have decided that is the choice, I guess we'll have to accept your resignation, but we hope you'll stay on the job for at least a couple of months until we find a replacement for you. This church owes you a lot for your long service, and our committee agrees you should be allowed to pick the day when your resignation becomes effective."

In more or less a normal and predictable sequence three days later the chairperson of the personnel committee received a letter of resignation from Sarah giving one week's notice, Don found a copy of it on his desk, the personnel committee countered with a decision to give Sarah three months' salary and benefits as terminal leave, Lillian Dempsey filled in as church secretary while a computer programmer-church secretary was found, hired, and trained, and nearly five hundred people turned out for a farewell party for Sarah held at a hotel. (This was a larger crowd than had been present for the farewell dinner for Dr. and Mrs. Bennington, but relief was a prime motivation in causing some people to attend that event while the combination of relief, sincere appreciation, deep friendships, guilt, longer tenure, sympathy for a victim of technological change, personal obligation to Hank, and a lower price for the meal produced a bigger crowd for Sarah's farewell dinner.)

While several dozen of Sarah's friends felt she had been victim of a heartless conspiracy, most of the scapegoating was directed at (a) the computer, (b) members of the two ad hoc committees, (c) the personnel committee, and (d) the board. Don escaped relatively unscathed. Six months after the farewell dinner for Sarah, the Larkins announced that Hank was retiring and they were moving to make their permanent home at a house on a lake they had purchased several years earlier. Two years later the entire episode was almost completely forgotten. The computer had another victim, two ad hoc committees had shielded Don from damage he did not deserve, and peace had come to the office at First Church.

Earlier, on Pastor Johnson's second day as senior minister at First Church, the sixty-eight-year-old semi-retired minister of visitation caught Don for a few minutes and explained, "As you may or may not know, I told people here soon after I learned of Dr. Bennington's decision to retire that I was ready to leave. I told the personnel committee I would stay for a maximum of one year following the arrival of the new senior minister, but I'm ready to resign whenever it fits your convenience. You set the date and that will be that."

Don replied, "Let's not rush this. Can we wait another

month or two and allow me time to get acquainted with this place before we talk about your leaving?"

Two months later they agreed the minister of visitation would stay through Don's first year and depart the following summer. With the exception of the future of John Owen, the part-time choir director, Don now had the beginnings of a transitional staff he felt he could work with while he concentrated on other issues. Before moving on to those other issues, however, it may be useful to look at several other aspects of building a staff team.

The Deference Pyramid

One aspect of staff relationships that often is overlooked is the pecking order among staff members, or what is more politely described as the deference pyramid. While objections may be heard from those who are convinced an egalitarian society can be achieved by declaring it now exists, considerable evidence can be mustered to support the contention that people do defer to one another in predictable ways.

Among the most common patterns of deference are (1) for most of human history younger people were expected to defer to older people (this was more widespread in the 1950s than it is today), (2) people with limited tenure are expected to defer to those with more seniority (the United States Congress is one place where this has been challenged in recent years), (3) traditionally the laity have been expected to defer to the clergy (in recent years this has been challenged and still is more visible in the Roman Catholic Church than in Baptist circles), (4) traditionally women have been expected to defer to men, (5) employees have been expected to defer to the employer, (6) less well-educated persons are expected to defer to those with more formal education, (7) for centuries lower income people have been expected to defer to higher income people, regardless of age, (8) traditionally Blacks have been expected to defer to whites, (9) people with less impressive titles have been expected to defer to those with more impressive titles, regardless of age or seniority, and (10) part-time people are expected to defer to full-time employees.

While the deference pyramid is far less powerful today than it was thirty or sixty or ninety years ago, as both the United States and Canada have moved toward a more egalitarian society, and it is far less influential in North America than on other continents, the deference pyramid is a force to be reckoned with in academic circles, political parties, churches, military organizations, the delivery of health care, and youth groups as well as in most other social organizations.

People tend to be most comfortable when there is a high degree of internal consistency in the deference pyramid of an organization. Thus staff relationships in the large congregations usually display less internal disharmony when the senior minister is among the oldest members of the program staff, has the longest tenure, is male, has the most formal education, receives the highest salary, carries the most impressive title, and is employed on a full-time basis. (At least two dozen large congregations have experimented with a half-time senior pastor in recent years. One reason most abandoned it after a brief period was that the experiment ran counter to the deference pyramid.)

When internal inconsistencies in the deference pyramid are present, people tend to feel uncomfortable. Perhaps the classic example of this is the fifty-eight-year-old senior minister who holds the bachelor of divinity degree, has been serving this same congregation for fifteen years, insists on being addressed as "Jim," and is assisted by the twenty-seven-year-old associate minister who holds the doctor of ministry degree and wants to be addressed as "Doctor Jansen."

A parallel, but less humorous example can be seen in those smaller congregations where the twenty-nine-year-old, newly arrived minister finds a full-time, fifty-three-year-old church secretary of twenty years firmly in charge of that parish and not about to relinquish control.

A similar internal dissonance can be found in that congregation in which a forty-three-year-old woman is the newly arrived senior minister, the fifty-seven-year-old male associate minister is in his twentieth year, the sixty-one-year-old minister of music is in his thirtieth year on the staff, and the sixty-four-year-old secretary to the senior minister is in her fortieth year on the staff.

How do people respond to the deference pyramid? A common way is to pretend it does not exist, to assume that by definition all Christians are kind and loving people and to blame internal stresses and discord on "unchristian" behavior. Another is to assume that merit, hard work, and superior performance will completely offset the power of the deference pyramid. A third is for the new head of the staff (chief executive officer, commanding officer, city manager, senior minister, department head, bishop) to replace everyone so the new head of staff has the greatest seniority. A fourth is to replace older males with considerable seniority with younger females. A fifth is to attempt to make titles the most powerful single force in the deference pyramid and deemphasize the influence of tenure, age, gender, and other factors. A sixth is to use a combination of titles and compensation to offset tenure, age, gender, education, and other factors. The churches, like military organizations, hospitals, and academic institutions, have placed a great emphasis on attempting to make titles and academic degrees carry more weight in the deference pyramid than age, tenure, gender, competence, and income.

On a long-term basis competence, dedication, and/or skills in interpersonal relationships can become exceptionally powerful influences in determining one's place on the deference pyramid, but in the short term, age, tenure, gender, titles, formal education, race, and income continue to be influential forces. Likewise, while competence, dedication, and relational skills are important, people tend to be more comfortable when all the factors in the deference pyramid are internally consistent. Thus the lay leadership usually is more comfortable when everyone agrees the most valuable player on the staff team is the senior minister.

When the sixty-one-year-old and still highly competent senior minister with twenty years tenure is perceived as no more than the third most valuable person on the staff following that young, brilliant, personable, and highly productive associate pastor and the extraordinary creative minister of music who joined the staff five years ago, it is not surprising that many members are more relieved than distressed or surprised when two of those three depart unexpectedly.

While it may not be as powerful as it was thirty years ago, the deference pyramid should not be overlooked when examining the inner dynamics of staff relationships or in building a new staff team.

What About a Co-pastorate?

At one point in his early months at First Church Pastor Johnson contemplated the possibility of eventually combining the salary paid the semi-retired minister of visitation with the stipend paid Neva, the director of Christian education, and the salary Anne had received as youth minister and creating a position for a second associate minister. One reason was he thought it might be easier to work with two full-time colleagues than with two full-time and two part-time staffers. A second was with the salary for this new position First Church might be able to attract an experienced minister who would stay for at least seven or eight years. A third reason was that with the extra money it might be possible to create a three-person co-pastorate. One might be the preaching minister, one could carry the primary responsibility for pastoral care, and the third could be a combination program director and administrator.

Before leaving St. John's Don had mentioned this to a fellow pastor and had been told of a United Methodist congregation in suburban Orlando that was using a two-minister team with one specializing in preaching and the other serving as program director and administrator. Aware that the team executive model was being used in the business world and having been promised considerable freedom in building a new staff, Don was determined to look into the possibility of replacing the old model of a senior minister and two associates with a new three-person co-pastorate.

Within a few months following his arrival Don found that among the most active members at First Church was a man named Eric Stromberg. This thirty-eight-year-old member had earned a doctorate in business administration and, after teaching for five years, had established his own management consulting firm. Don made an appointment to go to Eric's home one Thursday evening to meet with Eric and his wife, Lana, who it turned out, had been a management consultant for several years before she and Eric had been married four years earlier. In addition to being the mother of two young children, Lana now was a partner in the firm her husband had launched back before they had first met.

After twenty minutes of getting-acquainted conversation, Don got to the point of this visit. "As you both are aware, I'm sure, the time has come for me to do some long-term thinking about the program staff here at First Church. One possibility is by combining some of the present positions we could end up with three full-time ministers, all at a decent salary level. That may take some time, but I'm looking down the road a couple of years. I've read a lot about the merits of a collegial model for a staff team, and I've also read about how a growing number of business corporations are now operating with a group executive team consisting of three to ten people instead of one person who is the head honcho. I came over tonight to pick your brains. What do you think of the idea that we build a three-person co-pastorate at First Church?"

"You called me to make this appointment for tonight," replied Eric, "but I think you really want to talk with Lana about this. She's had far more experience with the group executive concept than I've had."

"Well, first of all, Pastor," began Lana, "you should realize this is not a new idea. The concept goes back to the 1960s or earlier. Borden, the dairy company, installed the concept back in 1967 and, as far as I know, is still using it.

"Second," she continued, "you also need to know that for the past several years about as many companies are discarding the idea as are adopting it. Third, from my perspective, the greatest value is in a transitional period for a company. For example, if you expect to be here at First Church for only three or four years on the assumption this congregation has to make some radical changes in its role and direction during that time, I could see considerable merit in creating the troika you describe. That has been one of the concept's greatest values in the business world."

"Well, I came hoping I might spend the rest of my ministry here at First Church," replied Don, "and I don't see any radical changes immediately ahead for First Church. Why can't that model be useful for ten or fifteen years?"

"I can suggest at least four reasons right off the top of my head," offered Eric who clearly wanted to be a part of this discussion. "First as I understand its history in business, it is primarily a leadership model for a transitional era. Second, it is a response to a particular situation. Given the dynamic nature of institutional life, that situation probably won't prevail four or five years later. In effect, if you choose a staff team to guide an institution through a transitional state and they do that successfully, the new era may require a different leadership model and almost certainly will demand a different mix of skills, gifts, and capabilities from that leadership group. Finally, people change with the passing of time. Sometimes that means what originally was a well-balanced team may no longer be that five years later as interests and skills change. Likewise, it may be very difficult to maintain that team as an effective unit when one or two members depart. As every football coach and baseball manager knows, rebuilding a championship team involves a lot more than simply replacing three or four players."

"Perhaps the biggest hurdle you would have in attempting to install that concept at First Church is a combination of tradition, polity, and institutional culture," reflected Lana. "This is a big congregation that has always been organized with a hierarchical system and the polity of our denomination reinforces that hierarchical approach. If you wanted to install a co-pastorate in a church, it seems to me the best place to do it would be in a brand new congregation in which you would be creating a new congregational culture rather than inheriting one."

"But a new congregation can't afford three ministers," objected Don. "The only place we can experiment with the concept is in a congregation large enough to afford three pastors."

"That raises another question," added Eric. "While I don't believe this is absolutely essential, my hunch is if you want to build a team of equals, their compensation should be equal.

I'm not sure the people at First Church are ready to increase the payroll by $20,000 or $30,000 a year to bring in two new ministers at your salary level."

"Please don't think we're trying to discourage you," assured Lana. "All we're trying to do is to help you sharpen your own thinking on what you want to do. My impression is you came over here tonight, not to secure our approval, but simply to get our reactions. Is that right?"

"That's correct," replied Don. "I'm not at all sure at this time I want to push it. This is simply one alternative I've been thinking about and I hoped your experiences would raise questions I hadn't even thought about."

"Good, I'm glad we understand one another," continued Lana. "If you do decide you want to refine it, Eric and I will be glad to work with you. But before we can do that, we would need to know why you are considering it. If you want to use the concept as an executive model, I would suggest you forget it. My experience suggests it encourages procrastination and it's really a political tool. In the best teams I see the buck for decision making still stops at the same desk when push comes to shove. If you want to use it as a means of encouraging dialogue among the program staff and for soliciting advice in an open setting, I believe that will be a benefit. If you want to encourage the pastoral staff to consitute a mutual support group for one another, this would be one way to accomplish that. From my perspective the number-one reason I would advocate the group executive office would be if you expect to bring one or two more women to the program staff, either lay or ordained. Moving away from the traditional hierarchical model could be one way of accomplishing that, but it is not the only way."

"One thing you want to be cautious about," interrupted Eric as men tend to do, "would be to create the perception that you are designing an organizational structure to exclude the laity from having a powerful voice in how this church is run. You can do that, I guess, in some of those huge independent churches where the staff makes all the decisions, but First Church has a long history of a strong lay role. You run the risk of proposing a staff arrangement that could be perceived as a means of turning all authority over to the staff."

"There's something in what Eric says," conceded Lana. "Historically the greatest benefit in the business world from the group executive office goes back many, many decades. That has been to make it the long-range planning committee for the corporation and that has proved to be beneficial in many of the Fortune 500 congregations. At First Church, however, I'm not at all sure the laity are willing to allow the staff to be our long-range planning committee. I believe our people want the laity to have a big voice in any long-range planning we do."

"As I think about your proposal for a co-pastorate," reflected Eric, "two questions come to mind. First, I believe the organizational structure should reflect goals. If your number-one concern is staff relationships, I agree you should try to determine what would be the best model for enhancing and undergirding staff relationships. If ministry to and with people is your top concern, maybe you should try to identify the model that you believe will facilitate that. If you think in functional categories and want to find people to staff such functions as youth, music, worship, missions, evangelism, Christian education, and administration, you may want a radically different model that gives each staff person clearly defined responsibilities. If you want to introduce some radical changes, you should pick the model that will be built around planned discontinuity rather than continuity. If your top priority is to enlarge the lay participation in planning and decision making, think in terms of a model that melds both paid staff and lay volunteers into one team. Actually, in a church as large as ours, you can't do that around a single focal point. You probably will need to go to a highly decentralized rather than a centralized staff model, if you want to expand meaningful lay involvement in planning and decision making. If you want to keep the planning and most of the decision making within the staff and focus on involving the laity in doing ministry, not administration, a highly centralized model probably would work very well."

"You also must recognize that if you build a closely knit co-pastorate of three or four or five program people," declared Lana as she interrupted her husband, "one price tag on that is that each time a staff person leaves, you must rebuild the team. That takes a lot of time and energy. In my experience most organizations find that the decentralized staff arrangement makes it easier to terminate the employment of someone who should leave and that departure will be less disruptive. The more centralized the leadership, the more disruptive it will be when the time comes to replace a member of that leadership team. It's sort of like the difference between divorcing your spouse or finding a new family physician when the old one retires."

"About the only thing I'm sure of at this point," protested Don, "is that my life would have been less complicated if I had stayed home tonight and watched television. I never realized this was such a complicated subject."

"I still have one more point I want to bring to your attention before you leave," added Eric as he sought to regain the floor. "My second question I would raise with you is who will identify and select the members of this three-person co-pastorate? If the basic responsibility for selecting them is in a committee, you may have a difficult time building a closely knit and compatible team. If you have the authority to pick their successors, that will greatly increase the probability that you will get the kind of personalities you want and need for this arrangement, but because you will choose each of them and because you will have seniority over each of them, they will tend to look to you as the leader of the team, not as a coequal. You will be at the top of what may turn out to be a comparatively flat deference pyramid, but the pressures of seniority and experience will tend to place you at the top of the pecking order."

"What if Anne Potter agrees to stay and be a part of this team?" asked Don. "She has seniority over me, and I didn't pick her."

"If you want her to be a part of this co-pastorate and you want it to be a full egalitarian team, that will mean overcoming the differences in role that now exist. Both she and the congregation have been trained ever since she arrived that she ranks number three in the pecking order among the three clergy positions on the staff. In addition, you're twenty years older, have far more experience, and you carry the title of being senior minister," explained Lana.

"The people here are just getting used to the idea of her being promoted to the number-two spot in that hierarchy. If you want to build a three-person co-pastorate, it would be easier to bring in two new ministers. I am convinced Anne is an exceptionally capable minister, but it's hard to change role in the same setting. It would be easier to create the arrangement you're thinking about with new people rather than with individuals who had been functioning in different roles previously in this same congregation. As a general rule it's easier to assume a new role in a new setting."

"If you want to keep Anne, and I strongly support that," declared Eric, "and you want her to be seen as a coequal, I believe she should receive the same salary you're paid, perhaps with a modest difference to recognize the difference in experience."

"Before you leave, let me reinforce one point Eric made a few minutes ago," added Lana. "Decide your priorities first. If you want the program staff to function as a planning team, the group executive office has considerable merit. If you want a highly productive group of staff members, pick a more decentralized model. That's a basic trade-off you have to make. You can build a closely knit and mutually supportive staff team or you can have a highly productive set of staff members, but you probably can't have both."

As he walked the half mile back to his home, Don Johnson reflected that the evening had been both enlightening and frustrating. He realized he had been romanticizing the concept of a three-person co-pastorate and had not faced the question of trade-offs. His dream called for a reduced number of people on the staff, a closely knit, highly centralized, and mutually supportive team, and increased productivity. As he walked home, he realized that was a dream. He probably could not have all three.

Don was correct in this conclusion, but under ideal circumstances he might have been wrong. As a general rule of administration, a centralized staff and high productivity are at opposite ends of the spectrum. This trade-off can be seen in government, business, larger parishes with a team of several clergypersons designed to provide ministerial leadership for seven to twenty small rural congregations, academic institutions, military organizations, and in large churches. Decentralization and high productivity tend to go together as do a centralized staff and good internal communication.

Like every broad generalization, however, this one has exceptions. The big and most highly visible exception in staffing large congregations has two facets to it. The first is that some people are more productive than others. Experts in the subject differ as to whether that ratio is 3 to 1 or 4 to 1 or as much as 6 to 1, but everyone agrees some people are far more productive workers than others. Farmers have recognized this fact for generations. It has been affirmed in the compensation system of hundreds of organizations as many people are paid either on commissions or on a piece-work basis. Every experienced senior minister has encountered this fact of life. In the same number of hours some people can accomplish three or four or six times as much as others accomplish in the same period of time.

Thus by a careful selection process Don Johnson might be able to create a highly centralized staff team that also is very productive. The law of averages is against that occurring often, but it can happen.

The second important facet of that issue of the productivity of staff is the huge difference in work environments. In addition to the differences between a centralized and decentralized staff, and the differences among people, several other factors are at work. These include the clarity of expectations, the method for resolving conflicts over priorities, the internal reward system, the availability of and the skill in utilizing secretarial help, the geographical distribution of the membership, and the system of congregational self-government (a small governing board usually is able to make major policy decisions more quickly than large boards, ad hoc committees often are more productive than standing committees, authoritarian leaders are usually more productive than laissez-faire leaders, et al.). In addition, some church offices are located and designed to encourage visitors to drop in and interrupt the work of the staff while others are located and designed to encourage each staff person to manage his or her time rather than to react to interruptions.

One of the trade-offs facing most senior ministers in

designing a model of staff relationships is this choice between productivity and centralization of the staff. Another trade-off is between decentralization of the staff and superior internal communication. As a general rule, unless a careful effort is made to offset this tendency, the more decentralized the staff, the more likely the internal communication network must be formalized, though it still may be criticized as inadequate.

Hierarchy or Hub and Spoke?

A second difficult trade-off surfaces when the number of program staff members exceeds three or four. Don Johnson inherited a model from his predecessor in which nine people on the payroll (associate minister, youth minister, DCE, pastor's secretary, church secretary, organist, choir director, and two custodians) all had direct access to the senior minister. This is common and can be described as the hub and spoke model. It was popularized in the early 1960s when Lyndon Johnson became president of the United States.[1] When adapted to the church it places the senior minister at the hub and each staff person is represented by a spoke with a direct connection to the hub. It is a highly popular model with the staff since everyone enjoys the privilege of being able to work directly with the senior minister. It is favored by many pastors who believe everyone should have the right of direct communication. "My door is always open" is a frequently heard statement from these senior ministers. It is an adaptable model since it is easy to add spokes. Many ministers began to use that model when serving a middle-sized congregation in which the paid staff consisted of a full-time secretary and three or four part-time people including a custodian, organist, and choir director. The pastor was expected to supervise the entire staff. When moving to a larger congregation, that minister often found it easy to add a spoke for the associate minister and another for the financial secretary. Before long the hub had six to fifteen spokes, each with a direct link to the senior minister.

The hub and spoke model of staff relationships also reduces the chances that bad news will be kept from the senior minister. It is a way to increase the chances the senior minister will be aware of all problems, both major and minor. Many senior ministers enjoy being at the center of staff life.

On the other side of the ledger it has obvious disadvantages. If often makes it difficult for the senior minister to delegate responsibilities to a team of two or three staff members without being a part of that newly created team. It usually produces many interruptions for the senior minister's day. It may mean no decisions that involve two or more members of the staff can be made during the senior minister's absence. It almost invariably means that some staff members will feel others are gaining unfair preferences in securing more time with the senior minister than they are granted. When a change in senior ministers takes place, this model naturally produces a slowing down in the decision-making process and sometimes that process is immobilized for many months. It often means the top priority on the senior minister's energies is managing that staff team and responding to pleas from the spokes, rather than conceptualizing a vision of a new tomorrow or initiating new ventures in ministry and outreach. It clearly demands many hours of the senior minister's time every week. The larger the number of part-time staff members and the smaller the proportion of full-time people, the greater the demands on the senior minister's time and energy. Very bluntly, the hub and spoke is not compatible with the utilization of several part-time staff specialists as suggested later in this chapter.

The most common alternative to the hub and spoke model is a hierarchy in which one staff member may oversee the work of several others. In this model the church business administrator may be responsible for the supervision of all the office and custodial staff while the minister of music oversees the work and arranges the schedules of several part-time choir directors and the organist. The program director (who may be an ordained minister) is responsible for the work and schedules of all the program staff, sometimes including the minister of music.

One reason this model is so widely used is that it reflects the hierarchical model of the church followed in many denominations for centuries. Another is the obvious advantage of reducing the amount of time the senior minister spends in "administration" and increasing the amount of discretionary time available to the senior minister. A third is usually, but not always, greater productivity. A fourth may be an increase in creativity since not everything has to originate with or be cleared with the senior minister. A fifth is that it often is compatible with and reinforced by the perceived deference pyramid. A sixth is that it spreads responsibility among several members and this increased responsibility may spark creativity, self-reliance, initiative and also result in longer tenure for many full-time staff members. A seventh is it clearly opens the door wider than the more highly centralized hub and spoke model for greater participation by lay volunteers in both planning and policy making as well as in doing ministry. An eighth is that it is highly compatible with the utilization of part-time lay specialists.

The obvious disadvantage is that most staff members prefer a direct relationship with the senior minister rather than being responsible to a "boss." Another is that some people are ideologically convinced hierarchy is a dirty word today. A third, and one of the most serious disadvantages is that the senior minister not only may be shielded from bad news, but also may be kept ignorant of things a senior minister must know to be fully effective.

The larger the congregation, however, the more attractive the hierarchical system appears to be when compared to the hub and spoke model. Among the strongest advocates of the hierarchical model of staff relations are the spouse and children of the senior minister.

One Big Family?

From a different perspective a widely used model of staff relationships is the family. It may be the best model. It may be a highly unstable model. Nearly everyone grew up in a family setting. That family setting had a life-long impact on most of us. Those who enjoyed a healthy, reasonably happy, and secure family environment probably will enjoy this model of staff relationships. Those who had an unhappy family experience as children may not be happy with this model.

In the typical staff meeting in which this model dominates relationships the senior minister accepts the father figure role and the pastor's secretary or the director of Christian education or the church business administrator or the program director may be the mother. The semi-retired minister of visitation is the wise and patriarchal grandfather. That staff may include an associate minister who is a gifted, personable, and productive worker and clearly makes the parents very proud. Another staff person may represent a brilliant child who has never been able to get it all together and while the parents still have great hopes, they fear this one may be a disappointment. A third and less talented staff member may symbolize the child who is not especially creative, but is a plodder and never leaves a job unfinished. That staff family also may include an adopted child or a stepchild and that relationship can be seen clearly whenever the staff is together.

In this model, which Don Johnson inherited from the fatherly Dr. Bennington, everyone has direct access to father, but many confide in mother more often than in father. The children tend to pair off and there is considerable sibling rivalry.

At one end of the scale of this model is the wise parent who both teaches and encourages while at the same time lifts up internally consistent expectations. The rules are clearly articulated and accountability is a part of family life. From the congregation's perspective the senior minister may be seen as an overly protective parent while the staff may perceive the senior minister as a person with very high expectations, who encourages, supports, teaches, and comforts but does not always insulate them from criticism.

At the other end of the scale is the senior minister who is perceived by the staff as a distant and often cold father figure who may leave the staff members feeling like orphans. This father may reprimand rather than praise, demand rather than coach, talk rather than listen, and frown rather than laugh. When this is the model of staff relationships, it is not unusual for staff members to leave when the first attractive opportunity comes along.

When a new senior minister arrives where this has been the

operational model, some of the staff members may see this person as a new and unwanted stepparent or as an intruder. As Don Johnson used this conceptual framework to reflect on the situation he had inherited at First Church, he was able to depersonalize some of his experiences with the staff. Dr. Bennington apparently had perceived Anne Potter as his "little girl" and treated her like a favorite child. Don saw Anne as an adult and fellow minister and that "promotion" won him Anne's strong respect.

Neva, the director of Christian education, was a highly dependent personality and this made Dr. Bennington feel needed. Don came with a far stronger ego, a much greater goal orientation and found Neva's performance unacceptable. Dr. Bennington's primary goals appeared to Don to have been to (a) maintain harmony within the staff, (b) try to make everyone happy, and, last, (c) hope that everyone on the staff would be happy and effective in his or her work, but those first two goals apparently dominated his style of leadership. One of Don's goals was to have a more comprehensive and effective ministry of Christian education. As a psychiatrist who also was a long-time member at First Church explained to Don several years later, "The difference between you and Dr. Bennington is that he wanted this to be one big happy family, and you want to strengthen the ministry and outreach of this church. He wanted the staff to be happy and successful. You want First Church to be faithful and obedient to God's will. Those can be overlapping goals, but they are far from identical!"

Earlier this same member had explained to Don, "Sarah Larkin had been the secretary here for several years when Dr. Bennington arrived. He didn't pick her, he inherited her. When he followed the family model for staff relationships, he became 'Big Daddy' and that fit his personality and gifts. He was and is a kindly, generous, and easy-going father figure. He didn't choose Sarah, she was already here, as I said, and she became the mother, but in this case a strong and domineering mother figure. Dr. Bennington did 98 percent of the getting along with Sarah in that relationship, although she was willing and able to do most of the getting along when it came to relating to strong male lay leaders. There was no way in the world Dr. Bennington could have fired her. It would have been easier for him to divorce his wife, who dominated their marriage. He had a strong wife at home and another strong wife here at the office. My hunch is if the position had been vacant when he arrived, Dr. Bennington would have gone out and hired a strong woman as the church secretary. His satisfactions at home came from his relationships with their two daughters and he repeated that here with Anne and Neva. He never had a son and he never learned how to relate to that young associate minister who left before you arrived. That kid needed coaching, direction, and encouragement, and Dr. Bennington simply did not know how to provide it. I'm convinced that one reason he sought to be Dr. Bennington's successor was partly to gain a superior place on the deference pyramid with Sarah, who had treated him like an incompetent stepchild, and also because from his perspective he saw himself as far more competent than Dr. Bennington."

The senior minister who either inherits or chooses this model of staff relationhips will benefit from (1) a good grounding in family systems theory,[2] (2) having been reared in a family setting that included healthy father-child relationships,[3] (3) not underestimating the power of a pat on the back, a hug, a handwritten note of appreciation, a word of public recognition, and (4) recognizing that every model of staff relationships has both advantages and disadvantages.

The Mentor-Student Relationship

From a more limited perspective many senior pastors as well as a significant proportion of newly arrived associate ministers use the major professor in graduate school and the graduate student relationship as the model that describes their relationship. The experienced mature, wise, and successful senior pastor is seen as the mentor and the younger associate minister who recently joined the staff is the self-identified student or resident, to use a medical analogy. By definition this is seen as a short-term relationship, and it is not uncommon for the senior pastor to brag about the "graduates" of this model.

While it has many advantages it does have some disadvantages. The most obvious is that the number-one client is the new associate minister, not the life, ministry, and outreach of the congregation. Many congregations cannot afford the role of providing a post seminary apprenticeship. A second is that it tends to produce short tenure. That is part of the definition of the model. A third, and rarely mentioned potential problem is based on a study of 1,318 adviser-advisee pairs conducted by the psychologist Srully Blotnick. Blotnick found that only 27 percent of these adviser-doctoral candidate relationships were satisfactory, both personally and professionally, to both parties. When limited strictly to professional relationships, only 41 percent of the pairs described this as a satisfactory relationship.[4] All too often the mentor-student relationships deteriorate into an adversary situation. That may help explain why in multiple-staff churches this model tends to produce a high turnover among the ministerial staff. Finally, the rest of the program staff may see this close relationship between the senior minister (mentor) and the associate pastor (student) as one that excludes them or makes them into second-class citizens similar to the feelings expressed by many undergraduates in large research universities.

The Boss-Subordinate Model

While some senior pastors and a great many associates are philosophically opposed to this concept, a common approach to staff relationships is the boss-subordinate model. This can be seen frequently in the relationship of the business administrator to the custodian staff, in the relationship between the senior pastor and the church secretary or the relationship between the administrative assistant to the senior minister and members of the clerical staff. Many associate ministers who entered seminary after fifteen or twenty years in the business world see this as a comfortable model when they join the staff of a very large congregation following their graduation from seminary. Perhaps the most hostile reactions to this model come from some of the retired military chaplains who become associate ministers following two or three decades of military service and insist on the role of colleague rather than subordinate.

Like every other model discussed here, this one has both advantages and disadvantages. Perhaps the chief limitation is that it probably will not be a constructive model unless everyone on the program staff, both lay and ordained, is somewhere between willing and eager to follow it. From this observer's experiences the five groups most likely to resist it are (1) retired military chaplains serving as associate ministers, (2) senior ministers who are unwilling to accept the role and responsibilities of functioning as "the boss" (this may be the critical point that almost guarantees failure for this model), (3) staff members who are philosophically convinced the Christian churches should model egalitarian relationships rather than hierarchical systems, (4) ordained staff who believe the professional ministry should be a brotherhood of equals, not a superior-subordinate relationship, and (5) perhaps one-third to one-half of all professionally trained directors of music.

The advantages include the clarity of the lines of accountability, the clear structuring of the role of the senior minister as coach, encourager, motivator, supervisor, teacher, final authority and the compatibility with the operational polity of many denominations. The polity of the Roman Catholic Church, the Episcopal Church, the United Methodist Church, thousands of Baptist congregations, many large independent churches, and the tradition of many black congregations support the boss-subordinate model. Many lay leaders prefer it because it is easy to comprehend, to explain, and it eliminates many questions about accountability. "If the buck stops at the desk of the senior minister, that person should have the authority commensurate with that responsibility." The laity, more than the clergy, appear to recognize the merits of placing both authority and accountability in the same person. (This also may help explain the disproportionately large number of unhappy associate ministers in The United Methodist Church.)

Perhaps the chief disadvantage of this model reflects the fact that it is ideologically unacceptable to a growing number of highly competent, remarkably creative, and self-directed individuals who are far more comfortable in the role of ministerial colleague rather than subordinate. This trend is reinforced by the fact that with the notable exceptions of the Roman Catholic Church, the Episcopal Church, and the Southern Baptist Convention, few religious bodies are preparing clergy to serve as part of a multiple staff.

A second disadvantage, as mentioned earlier, is the unwillingness of many senior ministers to accept the role and responsibilities of "the boss." The most subtle disadvantage is that it may encourage excessively long tenure among some staff members who come to enjoy that comfortable dependency relationship. While this may have some advantages in terms of both harmony and productivity, it may inhibit creativity. In addition, after a couple of decades in this setting some of these dependent staff members may encounter great difficulty when they do seek to move.

A fourth, and frequently disruptive disadvantage is it may be difficult to find two consecutive senior ministers who are both able and willing to fill that role as "the boss." Like the highly centralized staff team, it is more difficult to replace people after they depart.

Perhaps the biggest advantage of this model is that it eliminates a frequent source of confusion and conflict. Should a subordinate staff member's *primary* loyalty be to that congregation or to the senior minister? This model answers that question very clearly. The primary loyalty of the subordinate is to the boss, not to the organization! As a general rule the more clearly delineated the distinction between personal and institutional loyalties and the more widely that distinction is understood and supported, the easier it is to create a harmonious and productive staff team.

The tension created by this model can be seen most clearly in these numerically declining congregations in which several strong and influential lay leaders seek a senior minister who will lead the congregation in reversing that numerical decline and the widespread dislike among both the clergy and lay program staff members for anything that resembles a superior-subordinate model. This is also a conflict between those who see the central issue as results versus those who place great importance on choosing the means, in this case the model of staff relationships, that is expected to achieve the desired results. The laity are more likely to evaluate these issues in terms of results while many staff members, both lay and clergy, are more concerned with interpersonal relationships, turf, and authority patterns.

What Is the Issue?

Before moving on to look at other models of staff relationships, it may be useful to inject another question at this point. What are the critical factors that produce a harmonious, productive, and creative staff team in which every member looks forward eagerly to what tomorrow will bring? Obviously the gifts, personality traits, expectations, skills, and experiences each person brings to the team will be powerful influences. The setting,[5] the context for ministry, and the work environment also are powerful forces in determining the nature and quality of staff relationships.

Perhaps the most widely neglected factors are perspective and priorities. This can be illustrated by contrasting two different perspectives. As he sought to reconstruct history, Don Johnson became convinced that his predecessor at First Church had conceptualized the staff as a collection of individuals, each with his or her own responsibilities who report to the senior minister and who should see themselves as members of one big happy family.

Don's conceptual framework began with a large and complex program at the center with many mutually reinforcing components. He saw himself as the leader of a staff team called to lead the congregation in fulfilling its ministry. He saw it as his responsibility to see the larger picture, to conceptualize and articulate purpose, direction, goals, program, events, activities, and experiences as components of that larger concept. He hoped every staff person would see his or her role as a valuable member of that team, not as the overseer of a separate kingdom, and would be driven by group, not individual, goals.

Don also was convinced that he had inherited a combination model in which the staff met weekly for an hour-long family reunion and departed, each to his or her own little kingdom.

Part of Don's dilemma was how to build a staff that would function as a team, produce the productivity of a highly decentralized staff, relate to one another as supportive members of a caring family, be motivated by identical visions of what God was calling First Church to be and to do, recognize their interdependence and the necessity of mutually reinforcing goals and activities, minimize the natural drift toward becoming a hierarchy, benefit from healthy internal competition but not become a network of rivals, and also offer challenging, fulfilling, and satisfying experiences for everyone on the staff.

In other words, Don was still not ready to face the inevitability of trade-offs. For him, as for many other senior ministers, the central trade-off parallels the one faced by the conductor of a symphony orchestra. Which is the higher priority, a superb performance or a happy and compatible collection of musicians? As Don eventually moved to the second phase of building a staff, he found himself placing the superb performance higher on his priority list than the happy and mutually supportive team. That meant he had to forget his dream of one orchestra with three conductors and accept the role as head of staff.

A parallel can be seen in America's military organization. During World War II the energizing force was to win the war; keeping the generals happy was a minor concern. For the next four decades the joint chiefs of staff functioned primarily as a collection of tribal chiefs, each determined to protect and expand his own tribe. Should the program staff of the large congregation be organized around the central goal of doing ministry or around the needs of the individual staff members? That may be the key question in choosing a model of staff relationships. A critical issue in choosing that model may be whether the senior minister chooses the role of manager or accepts the responsibilities of leadership.[6]

Other Models

In addition to the models of staff relationships identified previously dozens of other models exist. The range and variety can be illustrated by examining briefly a few of the more common models.

1. The academic model. In this model the senior minister functions in a role similar to the president of the four-year liberal arts college and is the symbol of the institution. Other staff members lead their own departments with a high degree of autonomy. Some of the larger departments may have an assistant to the department head and a couple of administrative officers relate directly to the senior minister. The department heads are accountable to the dean who may carry the title in the church of program director or of executive minister.

2. The military model. In this model the senior minister is the commander and the executive minister corresponds to the executive officer. Much of the oversight for both program and administration is delegated to the executive minister. This model can provide the senior minister with a huge amount of discretionary time every month.

3. The team of specialists model. This model usually calls for the senior minister to specialize in finance, administration, and personnel matters, while other staff members specialize in pastoral care, education, evangelism, missions, youth, community outreach, music, and other program areas. One of the basic responsibilities of the senior minister, in addition to preaching and recruiting highly competent staff members, is to keep this array of specialists moving in the same direction toward a common goal at approximately the same pace.

4. The competition model. This is a very common model in which all program staff members see themselves in competition with one another for (a) the senior minister's time and support, (b) money, (c) lay volunteers, (d) visibility, (e) affirmation, (f) space, and (g) favorable dates on the calendar. One common product of this model is that the senior minister often becomes an overworked and weary referee. A second is that when a lay volunteer who is heavily involved in the missions program rejects an appeal from another staff person to give time to that program, the response, in words chosen to induce guilt, may be, "But this is the fourth time I've asked you to help me and you keep turning me down. Don't you like me or do you feel my program is not important?"

5. The team of teams. This model may resemble the hub and spoke model and is most often found in churches that have a dozen or more program staff members. The senior minister is at the hub, and each of the team leaders of the several program teams reports directly to the senior minister who also may occasionally attend a meeting of one program team.

6. The winner-loser model. This is most widely utilized when the time has arrived to add another position to the program staff. The persons on the program staff divide up among themselves those responsibilities that (a) they feel competent carrying out, (b) they enjoy doing, and (c) they want to do. The remaining responsibilities, which consist of what no one wants to do and/or no one knows how to do, are combined into the job description for the new position that is about to be created. Frequently an inexperienced person who just graduated from theological seminary is brought on staff to do what the experienced staff members do not know how to do or do not want to do.

7. The mutual support group. A substantial number of senior ministers seek to build a mutual support out of the program staff. It soon becomes clear to the more perceptive staff members that their number-one responsibility is to support, encourage, help, comfort, love, and nurture one another. Ministry to one another is the top priority, ministry with members, largely on a one-to-one basis, naturally becomes the number-two priority and program is a distant third.

If the senior minister is in a troubled marriage, that may mean support of the senior minister becomes the number-one priority and the mutual support of one another becomes the number-two priority.

If, for example, this mutual support group is composed of four members and all except the senior minister leave within the space of a year or less, a common result is (a) an attempt to build a new mutual support team, which usually is unsuccessful, followed by (b) the resignation of that senior minister.

8. The rescuer model. A tiny minority of senior ministers use this model to build a staff. One associate minister is a pastor who had to leave that last church and was rescued by being offered a position on this staff. The church secretary is a mother who was devastated when her husband left her for a younger woman. She needed a job in order to pay the bills, she needed a loving support group, and she needed something to do to take her mind off her problems. The custodian is a self-identified ex-alcoholic who occasionally falls off the wagon and refuses to believe he is an alcoholic. One reason he knows he is not an alcoholic is that he is convinced no church would hire an alcoholic as the custodian. The other associate minister is semi-retired after serving eighteen different churches over a period of thirty-five years. The goal is to offer him one rewarding, "successful," and satisfying pastoral experience before he retires. The financial secretary was fired by a local savings and loan association for embezzling money and pleaded for "one more chance."

One senior minister who intentionally uses this model explains, "The name of the game for a Christian congregation is redemption! Look at who Jesus picked to carry on his work. Most senior ministers never would hire six or seven out of the twelve. We make it with about half and it usually turns out we can't help the other half, but we can't predict in advance who will be in which half. As long as I'm in the ministry, I'll continue to be convinced that every church should see itself as a redemptive community and I'll try to put that into practice wherever the Lord calls me to serve."

9. The rotating chair. As part of the larger effort to build a collegial model or something resembling the group executive office discussed earlier, a relatively small number of senior ministers ask program staff members to take turns chairing the weekly staff meeting. One goal is to symbolize equality. Another is to expand the range of experiences for each staff member. A third is to force everyone to experience the perspective that goes with chairing those meetings.

A delicate point in determining the success of this model is the agenda. If the agenda for each meeting is prepared by the senior minister, it soon becomes apparent to everyone the senior minister remains in control, regardless of who chairs that weekly staff meeting. If the person chairing the staff meeting prepares the agenda, the result may be considerable discontinuity. Some staff members may arrive and discover an item of great concern to them that was to be carried over from last week is not on this week's agenda. If the first order of business following the devotional time is to prepare an agenda, the task-oriented members of the staff may become highly impatient about the amount of time devoted to that exercise in participatory democracy.

This model assumes continuity, habit, tradition, the deference pyramid, and performance are less influential and less important than enhancing staff relationships.

While this is far from a comprehensive list of models, it does illustrate the existence of a broad range of choices. For those so interested several systems exist for dividing the range of models into two or three categories. One system suggests the staff model will focus either on doing ministry and performance or on enhancing the quality of staff relationships and all models fall into one of those two categories. Another conceptual framework assumes the primary emphasis is on either relationships or functions. A third approach for dividing up the world argues all models of staff relationships fall into one of three categories, (a) the primary focus will be on taking care of the needs of the staff, (b) the primary focus will be on taking care of the members, or (c) the primary focus will be on evangelism and outreach. One denominational executive who uses this conceptual framework in looking at models of staff relationships insists she usually can identify the model being used by listening to the words of the prayer that opens the staff meeting.

Another denominational official who has worked with many large multiple-staff churches contends that all models of staff relationships are concerned with power and control and how power is distributed. He contends all models fall into one of two categories, (a) the maximum degree of control is retained by the senior minister, or (b) power is distributed among all members of the staff.

What is the central dynamic for the model of staff relationships used in your congregation?

Will It Be Different?

It appears that a growing number of people are convinced that new models of staff relationships will evolve with the increase in the number of women holding the position of senior minister. (In mid-1987 this writer had been able to identify less than one hundred large multiple-staff churches in the United States served by a woman as the senior minister. Fewer than one-half of these congregations were affiliated with one of the old-line Protestant denominations.)

Nearly everyone agrees that every social institution is affected by ideological considerations and values. The differences that will come in staff relationships with the increase in the number of women serving as senior ministers are yet to be determined. The experiences of women as elementary school principals, hospital administrators, and military officers demonstrate women do not share a common leadership style. Thus far the greatest quantity of research on this subject has been conducted for, by, or in the armed forces. This research indicates that when the definitive studies have been completed, a long list of variables will have been identified including generational differences, social class, ideology, personality, family and marital status, rank or title, education, denominational affiliation, race, gender, age, birth order, and type of seminary attended. It also appears gender will be among the less significant factors in that list of variables. Surveys on voting clearly indicate that race, generation, and ideology are far better predictors than gender on how people will vote. In 1984, for example, exit polls indicated a vast majority of black women and self-identified feminists voted for Walter Mondale while over 60 percent of the rest of the women who voted chose Ronald Reagan.

Thus far United States military organizations have had far more experiences than the churches in integrating women into a previously all-male system. Some useful clues may be gained by examining that research.[7] While feminist theory has been widely used to speak to social institutions such as academia and politics,[8] feminist theory has yet to be focused on the role of senior ministers. This observer's experiences suggest that recent years have brought a sharp increase in the number of women serving on the program staffs of large congregations,[9] but this has not been accompanied by radical changes in staff relationships.

Positions or Roles?

"What would the ideal staff look like if you built the perfect staff team for a large church?" asked a friend who was the senior minister of a congregation averaging nearly seven hundred at worship on Sunday morning.

"I don't know, but I'm sure of one thing," replied Don Johnson. "It would be different for you than it would be for me. You're in a relatively new congregation that is much larger than First Church, and you and I are different from each other in our gifts, skills, and experiences. Those are three reasons why we would not have the same definition of an ideal staff."

"Oh, come on," urged his friend, "forget those differences and dream with me. What would be an ideal staff?"

One response, which might fit a long-established congregation averaging between four hundred and six hundred at Sunday morning worship with a mixture of both younger families and mature adults might resemble this configuration.

Such a staff would include a senior minister who would (a) preach on at least thirty-five or forty Sunday mornings a year, (b) serve as an initiating leader, (c) either carry the basic administrative load or make sure the staff includes someone who is a competent administrator, (d) possess the gift of foresight and accept the responsibility for looking five years down the road in order to anticipate problems before they grow into crises, (e) be able to build and work with a staff of highly competent people, (f) bury at least some of the dead, officiate at some of the weddings, make sure the importance of these powerful rituals is not neglected and understand the importance of the power, prestige, and authority of the office of the senior minister in rituals and ceremonies, (g) accept the role as the resident expert on the Christian view of death or make sure that role is filled, (h) accept the role of umpire-in-chief when the time comes for close calls on critical decisions, (i) make some of the hospital calls, (j) spend at least 30 percent of every month doing what that senior minister does most effectively, (k) create and repeatedly hold up a vision for tomorrow, and (l) become sufficiently proficient in the management of time so none of these are neglected.

The amount of time allocated to family, devotional life, study, travel, hobbies, ecumenical and community affairs, and exercise varies tremendously among individuals and generalizations are risky. The only two generalizations that are reasonably safe to offer on that expenditure of time are that when forced to set priorities most members of large congregations suggest that (a) a high priority should be given to family and personal devotional time and (b) that denominational involvement, ecumenical relationships, and community leadership are low priorities in the allocation of the senior minister's time and energy.

A great many laypeople place an extremely high value on the senior minister's ability to convey the impression, "When you have our senior pastor's attention, you know you have all of it!"

Filling Out the Staff

The balance of this discussion of an ideal staff is directed at roles and responsibilities, not discrete positions in a table of organization. Frequently one person will fill two or three roles and accept several responsibilities.

Typically the second most critical responsibility in staffing the large church is the secretary to the senior minister. Ideally this individual will be an extroverted person who enjoys being with people, is the hub of the internal communication network, is clear the number-one loyalty is to the senior minister, is a committed Christian, is very effective in the use of the telephone, is a productive worker who knows the church, is not intimidated by computers, and is not a member of that congregation. (That largely eliminates problems over compensation, loyalties, future termination of employment, and second guessing the current pastor.)

The third most valuable player is the program director. In

some large churches the senior minister accepts this responsibility. The program director oversees all program, with the possible exception of corporate worship, has the basic responsibility for the coordination and scheduling of events, experiences, and activities and also, in many congregations, is responsible for the oversight of all paid program staff, although some part-time persons may be directly accountable to someone else on the staff. This person should be highly creative with an active imagination, able to think in a time frame of at least two years, comfortable with competition and conflict, and someone who enjoys complexity. The ideal program director uses words such as redundancy, complexity, more, bigger, and exciting and is generally opposed to proposals to making life simpler or to cutting back on program.

Some will argue the second most valuable player on the team is the church mother. This is a role that may be filled by the administrative assistant to the senior pastor, an associate minister, a director of Christian education, a program director or a lay associate, or the church secretary.

What does the church mother do? She (and most church mothers are female) makes sure people get along with one another, listens to their problems, puts a bandage on wounds, thanks and praises people who need to be thanked and praised, kicks those who need that form of encouragement, makes those telephone calls other staff members thought were unnecessary, consoles the sorrowing, explains to people what will not work *here* in *this* congregation *now*, celebrates victories, keeps the peace among the factions, asks the right questions, makes sure the kneelers are in place for weddings, turns out the lights before going home at night, makes emergency repairs, helps the highly rational male volunteers minimize the number of relational mistakes they otherwise might make, and keeps things moving. Like most mothers, the top priority for the day is what is most pressing that day including concerns others place on her agenda. (By contrast, much of the time senior ministers can enjoy the luxury of setting their own priorities for their day.)

The church mother makes a variety of emergency calls every week, helps the governing board distinguish between the petty and the important, substitutes for the trusted volunteer who fails to appear for a vital task, hugs the lonely, cheers up the despairing, and helps everyone find a long-term perspective in a moment of distress.

One woman who is the chief executive of a large corporation contends that child-rearing teaches the arts of compromise, conciliation, and listening and also provides good training in crisis management.[10] Those comments help explain how the church mother can help the big ecclesiastical organization become a reasonably happy home.

The extroverted greeter is a crucial role in the large congregation as well as in any congregation that has a substantial number of visitors on Sunday morning. This person enthusiastically greets at least two or three hundred people every Sunday morning, calls most of them, including first-time visitors, correctly by name during that brief conversation, hugs those who need a hug, affirms those who badly need affirmation, and receives and processes many nonverbal messages about what is happening in that congregation. In perhaps one-fifth of all large churches the senior minister fills this role, in another quarter the church mother or the minister of visitation (who may be one person with two roles) does this, in 5 percent someone else accepts the responsibility, and in perhaps one-half of all large congregations this role is currently vacant.

The backup ordained minister is almost an absolute necessity when the average attendance at worship passes three hundred. This role may be filled by the associate pastor, the part-time semi-retired minister of visitation, the youthful youth minister, the program director, the minister (if ordained) of music, a member who is an ordained minister but currently in a non-pastoral position (such as a chaplain at the nearby college), or a retired minister who recently joined this congregation.

How it is filled is less important than the fact that a backup ordained minister is available when the senior minister is not around for emergency hospital calls, funerals, weddings, and a variety of priestly acts. Usually it is relatively easy to find someone to fill the pulpit when the senior minister is absent, so typically that is not the number-one reason for filling this role. In some large congregations there is a recognized need for two backup clergy so the people have a choice when the time comes to turn to a pastor. In at least one-third of all multiple-staff congregations this is a highly demanding and full-time role because the senior minister does very little in the field of pastoral care. In many of these churches that highly skilled and heavily person-centered associate pastor may offer more continuity to congregational life than is provided by the task-oriented senior minister.

At this point it should be added that an important responsibility of at least one of the full-time program persons is to guard the senior minister against surprises, especially those that could turn out to be embarrassing surprises.[11] This responsibility may be carried out by an associate minister or by the church mother or by the whole staff, but it is important that someone do it. One of the most effective means of undercutting the ministry of the senior pastor is to permit an excessive number of surprises to occur every year, such as, "Oh, didn't you know Harry died Tuesday morning?" or "Oh, didn't you know our bank balance is down to zero?" Or, "Oh, didn't you know that couple has separated?" An excessive number is one.

The newest and fastest growing specialized role for the staff of the larger congregation is the church nurse. An excellent introduction to this role can be found in the words from a poster distributed by the Illinois Nurses Association. See poster on page 81.

Change one or two words and that becomes an excellent introduction to the proposal to add a church nurse to the staff of the large congregation. In earlier times churches organized hospitals to care for the ill. Today, as more and more churches identify themselves as wellness centers, the position of parish nurse is being added to the program staff. (In several communities this is a joint venture of several small congregations.) Dozens of large congregations, many of them in Ohio, Indiana, Illinois, Iowa, and Minnesota, have found this to be an important addition to the program staff.[12]

The church nurse, more often than not, is a part-time position, carries a broad range of responsibilities that may include classes on nutrition, calling on persons recently

Today, we need someone who can help us manage our health care needs in the hospital, the home, the HMO, the school, the workplace, in long-term care and in the community. Today, we need a provider who can teach us how to stay physically and mentally healthy and how to prevent illness and disease. Today, we need access to specialty practitioners who can provide expert health care for individuals and their families. Today, more than ever, we need an advocate who can deliver quality, cost-effective care throughout all the stages of our lives.

Today, We Need a Nurse

discharged from the hospital, listening, teaching a class for prospective new parents, counseling, encouraging people to see a physician, and diagnosing unhealthy patterns in staff relationships. Frequently this position wins strong and active support from the local hospital and a few hospitals are now offering training programs for nurses who see this as a new vocational possibility. As churches see the close relationship between health and one's spiritual journey, the number of ministers of health will increase.

Another key responsibility is the staff person who can build and oversee a network of volunteers. This includes identifying, enlisting, training, placing, supporting, and rewarding volunteers. The rewards vary from a hug to a letter of gratitude to public recognition to not being overloaded.

This is the person who, when volunteers are asked to come to the church to work, makes sure there are no frustrating surprises. If the task is to stuff envelopes, everything is ready so the volunteers can go to work immediately. If a volunteer is to go out and purchase food, the check to cover the cost has been prepared and is ready or, better yet, has been mailed or delivered to that volunteer. If the responsibility is tutoring a group of children, training experiences have been offered in advance.

This role may be filled by the administrative assistant to the pastor or the church mother or an associate minister or a specialist in working with volunteers, but it should be seen as a responsibility that requires skill, foresight, planning, and an ability to protect the vulnerable who cannot say no. This role also may include leadership development responsibilities. It always includes a willingness to work at expanding that network of volunteers.

Finally, in building that perfect staff, consideration should be given to finding persons who can accept these roles and responsibilities.

1. Building and overseeing a system for the assimilation of new members.

2. Building and overseeing a system for the enlistment of new members.

3. Building and overseeing a package of ministries with families that include teenagers.

4. Building and overseeing a package of ministries with families that include elementary school age children.

5. Building and overseeing a package of ministries with families that include young children.

6. Creating and overseeing a variety of opportunities that challenge people, regardless of age or marital status, to be involved in doing ministry.

7. Overlapping all of these, a staff person who can create and offer a variety of events and experiences that will help people, regardless of age, gender, marital or family status, to grow in their understanding of God's love and grace as they continue on their journey of faith.

8. Developing and operating a system for the electronic processing of both membership and financial data.

9. Developing, overseeing, and staffing, including the enlistment of part-time staff, a music program that includes a variety of groups, choirs, experiences, learning opportunities, events, and experiences. (See chapter 3.)

Instead of seeking one person to specialize in one role or to carry a single responsibility, this approach is based on the assumption it may be more effective to forget about positions, kingdoms, functions, job descriptions, and titles and build a staff where all roles are filled. Usually one person will fill three or four roles and carry several responsibilities.

Every system has its price tags and this emphasis on roles and responsibilities, rather than positions and job descriptions, is not an exception to that generalization.

The most obvious is a strong emphasis on families, not individuals. This is based on the assumption that (a) the churches should reinforce the place of the family in our society, (b) the family is the most influential educational force (with the possible exception of television) in our society, and (c) more can be done to help youth and children by working within a family context than by focusing on individuals. This emphasis on families is guaranteed to arouse (a) a negative response from those who contend the churches should be more sensitive to people who are not married, (b) support from those who have concluded "single" is somewhere between an obsolete program concept and a dirty word, and (c) questions from those who urge that the primary focus in organizing new programs should be on ministry, not marital status or age.

A second obvious dimension of this approach is a greater emphasis on roles and relationships than on functions. This tends to frustrate those who want a complete job description for every staff member as they think in terms of jobs rather than roles. As a general rule it also should be added that the greater the emphasis on roles and responsibilities, rather than positions and titles, the larger the proportion of the program staff who will be (a) part-time, (b) lay, and (c) female.

Although it is more common in some denominational families than others, scores of churches and ministers have discovered one approach to securing competent and specialized part-time staff is for one minister to serve as the part-time pastor of a small congregation while concurrently serving as a part-time staff member of a large church a few miles away. Experience suggests this may become a widely used concept.

The Growing Number of Lay Professionals

A third product of this change in perspective is already apparent. Congregations, not academic institutions, once again are becoming the primary place for training program staff members for large congregations. This is consistent and compatible, but farther advanced than a parallel trend that is for large churches to replace theological seminaries as the primary source for clergy. (Some readers will object that is not a new trend, but simply a return to the practices of the eighteenth, nineteenth, and early twentieth centuries when future ministers were trained by pastors rather than by professors.[13])

The emergence of this growing number of lay program persons serving on the staffs of large congregations also has provoked a debate over credentials and status.[14] A few denominations, such as the Lutheran Church-Missouri Synod, the Episcopal Church, and the Roman Catholic Church have a long and clearly established tradition of enlisting, training, and certifying lay professionals for work in the church. The status and role of these lay associates in ministry became a major point of contention in creating the new Evangelical Lutheran Church in America and a report is scheduled to be received in 1993. It also is a matter of serious concern in The United Methodist Church which receives the results of a major study in 1988. In several denominational families this is a relatively minor issue since the power to ordain rests with each congregation rather than in the denomination.

The requirements for certification and other facets of this issue are far more complex than they may first appear and vary tremendously from one denomination to another. For many the top item on the agenda is the distinction between being hired or called. If a person is called by God to this Christian vocation, should that individual be called (or appointed) as pastors are called (or appointed) or should that person simply be hired by a congregation?

For others the central issue is one of staff relationships. Does the lay associate work *with* the pastor or work *for* the pastor? Or does the lay associate work for the congregation? What is the number-one point of loyalty? To the senior minister or to that congregation?

Back in the days when the deaconess was the highest status vocation in the church for women and was formally called by the congregation, the issues were less confusing!

Should the money paid to lay associates for housing be exempt from the federal income tax—as is the housing allowance for pastors and for called teachers? Where is their place on the deference pyramid? What are the appropriate titles? Should their names be carried as "rostered personnel" in the denominational yearbook as are the names of all clergy? Should the diaconate be one step on the road to ordination or is it a destination? Should they be voting delegates to the annual meeting of the regional judicatory? What are the requirements for certification? Will these requirements emphasize academic credentials or skills and experience? Should lay associates be entitled to wear distinctive garb? Where is the primary point of accountability? To that congregation or to the body that provides the credentials? Should the ritual of certification be conducted in the home church or at the annual meeting of the regional judicatory? Does the regional judicatory have either the right or the obligation to intervene when the lay associate is being involuntarily terminated by the congregation? Is the primary support group for the lay associate in the staff or in the employing church or with a group of lay associates or with a group of volunteers in that church? Since the vast majority of certified lay associates are women, is sexism an issue? Should the regional judicatory adopt a minimum level of compensation, as is frequently done for the clergy? Which of the priestly acts can they perform? (Weddings? Funerals? Baptisms? Preach? Officiate at Holy Communion?)

What Will It Cost?

One Tuesday evening during that crucial first year Pastor Don Johnson met with the personnel committee to discuss alternative approaches to building a program staff. One of these was Don's earlier idea of upgrading the position of youth minister, originally filled by the Reverend Miss Anne Potter, to associate minister.

As he finished outlining that possibility the first question came from a man on the committee who asked, "What will it cost? We've been paying Anne a cash salary of $19,000 plus $4,000 for a housing allowance plus pension, health insurance, continuing education allowance, and convention expenses. If we upgrade the position, what will that cost us?"

"Well, that depends," equivocated Don, "on how much we increase the salary and whether we provide a church-owned house or pay a housing allowance. My guess is we will need to raise the salary by at least $8,000 to secure a competent and experienced minister, and, if we provide housing, that will raise the cost some more."

"Let's assume we do pay a cash salary of $28,000 and we purchase a house of $150,000 instead of paying a housing allowance," calculated this same member as he began to add some numbers on a piece of paper. "That means it will cost us $15,000 for the interest we will not receive on that $150,000 expenditure for a house plus utilities plus general property taxes plus insurance plus maintenance of the house plus health insurance plus pension, continuing education, convention expenses, and reimbursement for travel. That adds up to a package of between $53,000 and $57,000 for that position, and we haven't even begun to talk about secretarial help or other office expenses. That's almost double what it cost us to bring Anne on the staff."

"Well, I hadn't realized it would cost that much," responded Don. "Maybe we should look at other alternatives before we make any decisions."

It is impossible to make precise statements about the compensation of program staff in large congregations. Salary levels vary widely within denominations and regional differences also are significant.

Basic Generalizations

Seven generalizations can be offered, however, that do apply in most situations. The first, and the one that is almost universal, is the senior minister will receive the highest cash salary of anyone on the staff. Exceptions do exist, but they are rare. In at least 97 percent of all large congregations the senior minister's place at the top of that deference pyramid is both illustrated and reinforced by the salary schedule.

The second generalization is that the compensation paid the senior minister usually establishes a ceiling for salaries paid other staff members. If the salary paid the senior minister is low, other salaries also will be low. If the salary paid the senior minister is comparatively high, that usually means relatively high salaries for at least a few other staff members.

The third generalization is there is a huge difference in how high or low that ceiling may be and often wide variations can be found within a single denominational family. In early 1988, for example, it was not difficult to find senior ministers serving Anglo congregations averaging 500 or more at worship receiving a total compensation package (cash salary, housing, utilities, pension, continuing education allowance, health insurance, convention expenses, and book allowance) as low as $35,000, and it also was not difficult to find others where that total compensation package exceeded $90,000 annually.

A fourth generalization is that an increasing number of large congregations have concluded it is both more economical and more productive to decrease the number of full-time clergy on the staff and to increase the number of lay program specialists.

A fifth generalization is that part-time lay program specialists usually cost less per hour of productivity than do full-time staff members, either lay or clergy.

A sixth generalization is that the general trend has been in the direction of equalizing staff salaries. As recently as the 1930s it was not common for the cash salary paid the senior minister to be four or five or six or even seven times the cash salary paid the associate minister. Thus the cash salary of the assistant minister often was in the range of $500 to $1,200 annually while the senior minister's cash salary was in the $3,000 to $6,000 bracket. Typically the fringe benefits received by the senior minister also greatly exceeded those granted the assistant minister.

Finally, in broad general terms, when compared to other members of the American labor force, the cash salaries paid senior ministers have not kept up with the increase in the general level of wages and salaries. This may be a significant factor in the compression of the salary schedules referred to in the previous paragraph. This was illustrated at a subsequent meeting of that same personnel committee meeting when the focus was on Pastor Johnson's compensation.

The procedure in many congregations calls for the initial recommendation on the minister's compensation to originate with the Pastoral Relations Committee. At First Church, however, the tradition was for recommendation for clergy salaries to originate in the Personnel Committee while the senior minister initiated recommendations on compensation for all other staff members. After consideration by the Personnel Committee all recommendations were forwarded to the committee responsible for preparing the budget for the coming year.

"Well, who wants to pick a beginning point for our discussion tonight?" asked the person chairing the committee. "You all know why we're here."

"I would like to suggest that we pay our senior minister at

the same rate of compensation my grandfather received when he was the senior minister of a downtown church in Spokane eighty years ago," offered Elaine Macalester.

"I don't know what your grandfather was paid eighty years ago," interrupted Hal Bender with a smile, "but I expect we can do a little better than that. After all, everybody's income has gone up substantially during the past eighty years."

"I don't agree," replied Elaine firmly. "I don't think we can pay Don any more than my grandfather received, in comparative terms, but that could be the beginning point for our discussion tonight. My brother, who also is a minister, and I have just completed a biography of our grandfather, and in 1909 he was paid a cash salary of $5,000 plus a house to live in, but no other fringe benefits. Of course, he and his wife received a few gifts plus the honoraria for weddings. I thought we might use that as a reference point for our discussion tonight. In 1909 my grandfather was the same age Don is now, so that takes care of the experience factor."

"What would $5,000 be in today's dollars?" wondered another member of the committee.

"I checked that out before coming tonight," replied Elaine, "and the Consumer Price Index at the end of last year was slightly more than twelve times what it was back in 1909."

"That means a cash salary of $60,000," calculated an accountant on the committee, "I guess that's in the ball park."

"Wait a minute," corrected Elaine, "that $5,000 cash salary was my grandfather's total cash compensation. He was given a house to live in, but no allowance for travel or utilities or pension or continuing education or health insurance or other fringe benefits. That's what we call 'the package' here at First Church."

"I told you we can do better by Don than that church did by your grandfather," interrupted Hal Bender again. "The package we're paying Don now exceeds $60,000."

"Please allow me to finish," continued Elaine. "I suggested we think in comparative terms. How much was a $5,000 cash salary in 1909? My brother and I checked that out too and this may surprise you. In 1909 a cash salary of $5,000 a year was ten times the average annual earnings for wage earners in manufacturing, nearly five times the average salary of all employees of the federal government, almost exactly twelve times the average annual salary of all public schoolteachers, more than five times the average salary of all postal workers, and nine times the average annual earnings of coal miners," explained Elaine as she read from her notes. "In 1909 $5,000 a year was well above the total net income of all physicians in private practice, and it was six times what that same church paid my grandfather's assistant minister who had graduated from theological seminary four years earlier. In 1909 the average cash salary of all ministers in the United States was $831."

"This is fascinating," observed the accountant who was making notes as Elaine read her figures. "If we were to compensate our senior minister at an equivalent level, in terms of the wages and salaries received by other people in the labor force, to what your grandfather was paid back in 1909 we would be talking about a total package of somewhere between $130,000 and $285,000 a year, depending on our choice of comparisons."

"That's right," agreed Elaine, "but remember, I said that maybe we cannot do as well by Don as that church in Spokane did for my grandfather. Hal, do you still believe we can pay Don more than my grandfather received back in 1908?"

"I really can't believe this," replied Hal Bender as he sought new ground to defend his earlier position. "Your grandfather must have been an exceptionally well paid minister back in 1909."

"Elaine's figures surprised me, too," explained Don Johnson, "but I knew about the general trend. I didn't know the details, but I've known for a long time that when compared to other people, ministers are not compensated as well today as they were back at the turn of the century."

"You don't have to go back eighty years to see that," added Elaine as she shuffled the papers in front of her. "My brother also gathered the figures for other years. In 1926, for example, our father, who also was a minister and in 1926 was younger than Don is today, was paid a cash salary of $5,200 plus a house as the senior pastor of a large downtown church. His assistant, who had graduated from seminary several years earlier, was paid $1,400 plus a house and the average salary for all Congregational and Methodist ministers was $1,826. That compared to an average salary in 1926 of $1,277 for public schoolteachers, $2,128 for postal employees, $1,247 for coal miners, and $1,309 for all wage earners in manufacturing in 1926."

"But you have to allow for the fact that today the clergy receive a lot more in fringe benefits than they did in 1926," interrupted Hal Bender again. "Even as recently as the 1950s very few churches reimbursed the pastor for car expenses, and health insurance is a big item today. The total of the fringes here at First Church for Don, including the housing allowance, travel, pension, health insurance, continuing education, and everything else add up to over $22,000 a year."

"That's true," interpreted the accountant, "but the fringe benefits for nearly everyone else in the labor force also have gone up substantially in recent years and often are equal to one-fourth to nearly three-quarters of the cash compensation when you calculate the cost of paid holidays, vacations, health insurance, pensions, sick leave, and other benefits. I have one client whose cost of the fringe benefits she gives her employees is just a shade below the actual payroll. In addition, I think we agreed many years ago that reimbursement for mileage is a cost of doing business, not a fringe benefit."

"Well, I also turned to kinfolk for help in preparing for this meeting," declared Pat Marshall. "My brother-in-law serves as the senior minister of a large suburban church and recently he attended a three-day seminar for senior ministers where the question of salaries came up. He brought this sheet back from that meeting. All the ministers were asked to list their average attendance at Sunday morning worship, their denomination, their cash salary, and their total compensation including salary, housing, pension, health insurance, and other benefits, but not vacation or the value of sabbaticals. The range is unbelievable! Here is one senior minister with an average attendance of 435, a cash salary of $38,000 and a total package of $53,000. Another reports an average attendance of 680, a cash salary of $82,000 and a total package of $106,000. A third lists an average attendance of

1,500, a cash salary of $32,000 and a total package of $48,000. Seven of the 33 on the sheet list a total package of over $75,000 and eight list a total package under $46,000. All except six of the churches are in the 350 to 800 bracket in average attendance, but there is practically no correlation between size and compensation. The last includes churches from nine denominations. No names were listed, but here is a pastor in the Lutheran Church-Missouri Synod in a parish that averages 500 at worship with a cash salary of $21,500 and just below that is a minister in a Baptist church averaging 600 at worship with a cash salary of $61,000 and a total package of $83,000."

This conversation illustrates the point made earlier. When compared with other members of the American labor force, Protestant ministers serving city churches no longer are paid as well as they were back in the first few decades of this century. The accompanying table reveals that in 1906 the average salary for all ministers serving cities with a population of 300,000 or more ranged between $1,400 and $2,940 annually for churches in several of the old-time Protestant denominations. Those were average figures in a day when workers in manufacturing averaged $506 a year, coal miners averaged $537 a year, postal employees averaged $921 a year, public schoolteachers averaged $409 a year, and the street railways paid an average annual wage of $662.

In 1906 the average annual salary of all ministers in the United States was $773, and it was not at all unusual for the cash salary of the minister of one of the "tall steeple churches" to be in excess of $4,000 a year.

Although these historical comparisons do not constitute the most important factor in setting the salary for senior ministers, they do illustrate three of the generalizations made earlier.

First, ministerial salaries have varied and do vary tremendously. For example, the average salary of Southern Baptist ministers serving in big cities in 1906 was $1,793. That compares to the average of $1,358 received by Southern Baptist ministers serving in cities of 25,000 or 50,000 population and the average of $334 a year paid Southern Baptist preachers serving outside of the principal cities of the day—and that is where the overwhelming majority of Southern Baptist ministers served in 1906.

SALARIES OF MINISTERS SERVING IN CITIES
WITH A POPULATION OF 300,000 OR MORE
1906

Denomination	Average Salary
Unitarian Church	$2,940
Presbyterian Church US	2,450
Universalists	2,362
Presbyterian Church USA	2,169
Congregational Church	1,938
Reformed Church in America	1,938
Protestant Episcopal	1,873
Southern Baptist Convention	1,793
Methodist Episcopal South	1,642
Northern Baptist Convention	1,580
Jewish	1,491
Methodist Episcopal	1,422
General Synod Ev. Lutheran	1,405
Disciples of Christ	1,326
Methodist Protestant	1,000
Ch. of U. Brethren in Christ	938
African M. E. Church	835
Evangelical Association	812
Ev. Lutheran Synodical Conf.	807
Society of Friends	710
AME Zion	698
Free Methodist Church	669
National Baptist Convention	605
CME Church	350

Source: *Census of Religious Bodies 1906,* Washington, D.C.: Bureau of the Census, 1910. Part 1, pp. 94-95.

A similar pattern could be seen among Presbyterians, Congregationalists, and Methodists. The average salary in big cities in 1906 was two to four times the average for ministers serving in small cities and villages.

Second, when compared to other people in the labor force,

salaries for full-time urban pastors are lower than they were sixty or eighty years ago.

Third, the egalitarian pressures of recent years have compressed that ratio between the highly paid senior minister and the much lower paid assistant pastor so by the late 1980s the ratio was more likely to be three-to-one or two-to-one. Thus if today the cash salary of the senior minister is in the $40,000 to $60,000 bracket, the number-one assistant minister's cash salary may be in the $20,000 to $30,000 range. If the associate minister has fifteen or more years of experience in the pastorate, a common pattern today, but relatively rare before 1950, the ratio may be closer to three-to-two.

In a few denominations, such as The United Methodist Church and the Luthern Church-Missouri Synod where the cultural pressures have kept a comparatively low ceiling on the compensation of senior ministers and/or the egalitarian pressures have been unusually strong, the ratio may be closer to four-to-three or six-to-five if both ministers have approximately the same number of years of experience. It must be noted, however, that both of those denominations have a relatively tiny proportion of congregations averaging 1,000 or more at Sunday morning worship (0.2 percent for The United Methodist Church and 0.5 percent for the Lutheran Church-Missouri Synod).

The other two big changes in the compensation for senior ministers are (1) the proportion of senior ministers who have two or three months free during the summer to lecture, write, read, study, and prepare sermon outlines for the coming year has shrunk drastically since the 1930s and (2) the Tax Reform Act of 1986 makes home ownership the only substantial tax shelter available to most middle- and upper-middle-class Americans. That legislation may mark the end of the centuries-old tradition of providing church-owned housing for ministers. For an increasing proportion of the clergy, home ownership, the pension of the spouse, the denominational pension, and Social Security have become the foundation stones in planning for their children's education and for their eventual retirement.

Finally, it must be acknowledged that the rising costs of

health care insurance have influenced both the criteria for selecting staff and for calculating the compensation for staff members. In those denominations in which all costs for health insurance for the clergy, but not for lay staff, are paid by the regional judicatory from benevolence giving that biases the system in favor of congregations turning to clergy for program staff positions. In those denominations in which the congregations directly pay the premiums for health insurance, the bias is to encourage congregations to seek staff members who are covered by the spouse's health insurance program or persons covered by Medicare. In many other churches the policy is to offer everyone the same basic fringe benefits. This means it may be more economical to employ a husband-wife team rather than two unrelated full-time persons or to employ one full-time program member rather than three part-time staff persons. As the costs of fringe benefits increase, the task of building and fairly compensating the staff becomes more complicated.

Where Does the Buck Stop?

One of the most difficult issues facing senior ministers is to determine when and how to intervene when complaints are lodged against a staff member. Before leaving St. John's, Don had concluded (a) he would minimize his role as a message carrier, (b) he would encourage parishioners to take complaints directly to the appropriate person, and (c) unless it was absolutely impossible, he would always support his staff. These generalizations helped him in many difficult situations.

"Pastor, either you do something about the way my daughter, Shelly, is treated in the youth group here or we're leaving!" exclaimed an irate mother of two teenagers as she accosted Don Johnson in a corridor at First Church one Thursday morning. "Up until we got this new youth minister Shelly went to the youth group practically every week. During her first two years in high school she really looked forward every week to being with the other kids. Ever since Barbara took over from Anne, she doesn't want to go. Her younger sister, Valerie, is getting the idea that she doesn't want to be a part of it either when she starts high school next fall. I want you to do something about it!"

"Well, I'm sorry to hear you and Shelly are unhappy with the program," replied Don, "but when Barbara Cook joined our staff, it was agreed that the new definition of her responsibilities would include ministries with families that include teenagers, not just the youth. She has considerable specialized training in family systems and is far more competent than I in that area. If you're unhappy, I suggest you talk directly to Barbara. This is her area of responsibility and therefore I believe you would be well advised to talk with her directly, rather than ask me to intercede."

"But you're the senior minister around here, aren't you?" challenged Shelly's mother in a belligerent tone of voice. "If you're the senior minister, you should be able to do something to make Barbara change her approach so all the kids will want to participate. My Shelly is not the only teenager here who doesn't like what's going on with the youth program."

"Yes, I am the senior minister," agreed Don, "but I'm not in charge of our ministries with families that include teenagers. That's Barb's responsibility. The way we're organized here that means you'll find it more productive to talk with her directly, rather then try to go through me."

As it turned out, Barbara Cook was not able to placate either this irate mother or the two daughters, and a few months later the whole family left for another church that was reputed to have a huge ministry with youth.

While Don, like many other senior ministers, had feelings of guilt, inadequacy, and regret when this family left, he was able to respond to the critics, "Well, maybe it's better they go where they can be happy, rather than remain here and be unhappy." The operational translation of that was, "If I have to make a choice between risking the loss of one family and undercutting one of my trusted staff members, I'll take the risk of that family going elsewhere. I try to support my staff. If I don't do that, I can't expect them to support me. I do try to delegate both responsibility and authority, but when the choice comes down to those kind of situations, I realize the buck does stop at my desk. That's why I need to work out a set of guidelines in advance. Otherwise, it's easy to be pressured into trying to placate an unhappy parishioner rather than to take a long-term view of what we're trying to accomplish."

Don was right, the buck does stop at the senior minister's desk; Don was right, it is important to support staff members. That often means a choice between attempting to placate unhappy members or publicly supporting that staff member. Occasions do arise when that clearly is an either-or choice.

Don Johnson was right in lifting up the importance of developing some basic guidelines well in advance of the emergence of a crisis. That is part of a classical definition of a professional. Professionals rely on guidelines, principles, rules-of-thumb, previous experiences, and basic generalizations while the non-professionals take each situation as it comes along and do not worry about consistency or long-term consequences.

Don Johnson also had lived long enough by that time to recognize this no longer is a world of permanent relationships. Once upon a time it may have been true that when adults united with a church, that was a permanent relationship that would last until either death or that member moved out of town. Today many adults see themselves on a religious pilgrimage and church membership is a wayside stop on that journey, not a destination.

Don also had been able to accept as a fact of life that the larger the number of members, the higher the turnover. His earlier years as the pastor of small congregations made it impossible for him to be happy about that basic generalization, but he now was able to understand some of the reasons behind that fact of life. The larger the congregation and the more rapid its numerical growth, the more entry points it offers new people, but that also results in a larger number of points of possible alienation. The larger the congregation and the broader the program, the greater the number of needs that can be met, but that also produces higher expectations and that means more potential for not being able to fulfill all those high expectations. The new minister of that small congregation is generously congratulated on that occasional superb sermon. The senior minister of the large congregation is criticized for that occasional bad sermon.

The larger the size of the church, the more influential are functions, ministries, programs, and events in the set of ties that bind people to that congregation and the less powerful are relationships with other people. The larger the number of members, the smaller the proportion of members who are related by blood or marriage to any one member. As a result, disappointment in one area of ministry in a large church can produce a departure, while in a smaller church similar disappointments are less common since expectations are lower and departures are less frequent since kinship and friendship ties are stronger.

While it still tore at his emotions, Don Johnson gradually was coming to the point where he could see wisdom and find comfort in understanding that the larger the congregation, the greater the proportion of members who really belong in some other church.

Finally, although he was reluctant to admit it, Don Johnson gradually was coming to understand that he really was the pastor of two congregations. One congregation was composed of the consumers of ministry. The other congregation, which was much smaller in numbers, was composed of the volunteers and staff who were *both* consumers and producers of ministry. When a conflict forced him to choose between the two, Don almost always sided with that second congregation. Whenever he failed to do that, he subsequently regretted the decision.

The Staff Retreat

"What's the best thing you've done to enhance your ministry since coming to First Church?" inquired a friend of Don's several years after Don's arrival.

"That's an easy question," replied Pastor Johnson. "In my second year we started having an annual staff retreat that runs from after lunch on Tuesday through lunch on Thursday. The first year we built the retreat on the Myers-Briggs Type Indicator test.[15] That's a tremendous tool to help each one of us understand ourselves a little better and also to understand why other people tend to respond as they do. We had a professor from the seminary come out on Wednesday that year and help us interpret it.

"By the next year we had our full staff on board, and we used the time to strengthen the sense of being a team called to do ministry as a team," continued Don. "The year after that our staff retreat was designed to be a review of where we as a congregation were going. For that experience we included six of our key lay volunteers in that retreat experience. The next year we tried to focus on how and where we should expand the total program. By the time we got to planning last year's retreat we had three new people on the staff so we used the DISC program as the tool for helping us understand ourselves better and our relationships with one another. That really helped each one of us focus on what we do best and was a very affirming experience. This year we are going to try to do some long-range planning."

The annual two- or three-day staff retreat has become an increasingly common tool for enhancing the quality of staff relationships, for integrating new members into the staff team, for self-examination, for program review, and for looking into the future. It is difficult to overstate the values of that time spent in building a new staff team.

Facing the Music

Chapter Three

"You might as well face the facts of life, Pastor," warned a long-time member of First Church as he and Pastor Johnson met and stopped to chat one day on the way out of the post office. "The only reason certain old sayings are carried from one generation to the next is because they represent an eternal truth. My dad, who's been gone now nearly thirty years, always referred to the music department of the church as the war department. The other night my wife came home from choir rehearsal and told me John Owen is resigning as choir director because you're not satisfied with his work. John's done a fine job for us as choir director for a good many years now. He's been able to keep the peace, but when he's gone, you better be prepared for a big fight over finding someone to take his place. Music is the most divisive thing in the church! I sometimes think we'd be better off without it, but I guess that's not possible in a big church like ours."

As he listened to this warning, Don realized he had heard the ministry of music described as the church's war department at least a hundred times during his years as a pastor. Until this very minute Don had been thinking solely in terms of replacing John Owen. One possibility he had been considering was to seek a full-time minister of music. He had not thought of this as a potential battleground, but as he walked back to First Church, he suddenly realized that John Owen's impending resignation was going to be a bigger battle than he needed right now.

From Don's perspective securing a letter of resignation from the part-time choir director had been much easier than he had feared. A few months after his arrival Don had stopped by John's music store and, finding no customers in the store, had suggested, "John, when you get time, I would like to talk to you about expanding our whole music program. In another year or two we may decide to go to two worship services on Sunday morning and my dream is to have two adult choirs, perhaps a twenty- to twenty-five-voice choir at the first service and a thirty-five- to forty-voice choir at the second service. In addition, I think we need at least a half dozen other choirs and music groups. When you have the time I would like to get together with you and talk about how we can turn that dream into reality."

John Owen, who was clearly intimidated by Don's aggressive approach, responded, "I agree that would be great if we could do it, Pastor, but we're lucky now when we have two dozen people show up to sing on Sunday morning. I just don't think we have enough people at First Church to build a thirty-five-voice choir, much less have two choirs."

"Right after I arrived, I checked the choir loft and we can seat at least fifty people there," continued Don. "I don't see any reason why we can't have at least forty people in the chancel choir. People who have been around for a long time tell me that back in the 1950s First Church had a choir that completely filled the choir loft. If we did it once, I don't see why we can't do it again."

"Yes, that's true," replied John. "I've been at First Church since 1958, and when I joined the choir a few months later, we did fill that choir loft on maybe twenty Sundays a year, but all but one or two of those people are gone. You have to remember that back in the early 1960s we had nearly twice as many people in church on Sunday morning as we have today. Our attendance has dropped by about half and so I don't think it's out of line that our chancel choir is only half the size it used to be. Maybe if we get back up to six hundred at worship, we can get the choir back up to thirty-five or forty."

John, who was a few years older than Don and had thirty years more firsthand knowledge of First Church than Don possessed, felt the new senior minister was trying to put him on the spot. "Two can play that game," thought John as he laid down his challenge that suggested the size of the choir was directly proportional to the size of the crowd at worship. "Reverend Hotshot," thought John to himself, "you come into my store and try to blame me for the size of the choir. If you can draw the crowds we used to have, I can produce a bigger choir."

"That's a chicken and egg issue you're raising," retorted Don. "Which comes first? The big choir or the big attendance? I think they go together, but if we're going to increase our attendance and get it anywhere back up to where it used to be, I'm convinced we'll have to go to two services, and we'll need an extensive music program with two adult choirs as part of that effort."

Two weeks later John asked for an early Monday evening appointment with Don. When he came into Don's office, he laid his letter of resignation on Don's desk and declared, "I have a hunch this may be the biggest contribution I can make to your dream of two adult choirs and a big music program. A couple of days after you stopped by the store a church out near where I live asked if I would like to be their choir director, and I've told them I would. My letter of resignation includes a thirty-day notice. I hope you can find someone who can build the two big choirs you want. During the past several years I've pleaded, cajoled, and practically gotten down on my knees to beg people with good voices to join our choir, and I'm ready to give up. You may be right. We may have the sixty or seventy members it would take to produce the two choirs you want, but I haven't been able to find them. I sincerely hope you can."

During the next few weeks four messages circulated among the members of First Church. The official version, which was produced by Don and the worship committee, was that John Owen had resigned as choir director to accept a similar position in another church. The unofficial one, which was circulated by a dozen members of the chancel choir plus a few of his friends and never directly denied by John Owen, was that the new senior minister had forced the choir director to resign. A third, which was as much a sign of relief as a message, could be summarized in one word, "Finally!" The fourth, which was initiated by several members of the choir and several dozen other members who were convinced First Church both needed and deserved a better and larger ministry of music, was the hope that the dawning of a new day was near.

Don's strategy had been relatively simple and not at all unusual. Instead of directly asking John Owen for his resignation and thus encouraging people to view it as a conflict of personalities, Don had chosen to challenge the choir director with a vision of a new day. When John concluded the challenge was beyond his capabilities, he resigned. If he had not done so, Don was prepared to keep the focus on the dream of a larger and more extensive music program. As more and more people at First Church bought that vision, one of two things would happen. Ideally, John Owen would be inspired to a higher level of performance and a new era would begin for both the ministry of music and First Church. The alternative was that the gap between the vision and John's performance would become apparent to more and more people, and this would produce a decision. John took the easy way out and found another position. One reason John did that was because for a quarter of a century he had been taking the easy way out of difficult situations.

Nothing Is Free Except Grace

John's resignation, along with those from Sarah and Neva, meant that Don felt he was more free to focus on two of his highest priorities, building a new staff and expanding the program. As he soon discovered, that was a naïve expectation. He still had to live with a series of impressions and rumors that now were circulating throughout First Church.

The most obvious was that the new senior minister really did not know how to get along with people as well as Dr. Bennington had and that was the reason for the sudden high turnover in the staff.

A second was that he could not get along with women. Although Anne tried her best to combat that one, the facts remained that two out of three of the staff resignations came from women. (A couple of people pointed out that six of the eight people on the payroll when Don arrived were women, but few picked up that point.)

A third was that the new minister was a dynamic and demanding leader who would not tolerate incompetence and it was about time First Church had a senior minister who was willing to face the music.

A fourth was that the new senior minister had his own secret plans and would not reveal these to anyone.

A fifth was that this middle-aged minister was having an affair with the attractive Anne Potter and that was why he was recommending that she be promoted from youth minister to associate pastor despite her age and lack of experience. (Don did not hear about this rumor until several months later when Mary told him.)

A sixth was that the part-time organist was the one who had persuaded Don to fire John Owen because she wanted to be both organist and choir director. Those circulating this rumor could "prove it" when she was asked to be the interim choir director following John's departure.

A seventh rumor was that Don had expected attendance to surge immediately following his arrival and when it did not, he had picked John Owen and the choir to be the scapegoat.

Although that is not a complete list, the lesson is clear. Becoming the new senior minister of a large and long-established congregation often is a far more complex calling than it appears to be on the surface. The paranoid members seldom take vacations.

One-to-One or Groups?

"We're big enough now that we should have a full-time professionally trained minister of music," advised one of the choir members as she and the six other officers from the chancel choir met with Pastor Don Johnson. During his first several months at First Church, Don had instituted the system of a twice-a-year meeting with the officers of the choir. This was part of a larger strategy of Don's as he taught himself the role of being a senior minister.

For the first twenty years of his ministry Don had practiced, and greatly enjoyed, one-to-one relationships with people. During his last three or four years at St. John's Church, Don had begun to realize that the combination of the growing size of that congregation, plus his increasingly tight schedule as the years rolled past, made it impossible for him to spend the time in those one-to-one relationships that he coveted. By the time he left St. John's to move to First Church Don had realized he must change his style of ministry and place a greater emphasis on meeting and working with groups of people, rather than attempting to relate to people on a one-to-one basis. First Church included too many people and the day contained too few hours for him to be able to concentrate on one-to-one relationships with the parishioners.

Don also had reached the point in his life journey that he realized he needed help if he was going to be successful in changing to a different style of pastoral leadership. He also had learned that one of his most effective tools would be the way he planned the use of his time. Therefore, as part of his personal strategy to force himself to change ministerial styles, he had taken control of his own schedule. After two decades of reacting to the demands, schedules, and whims of others, Don had, by the time he left St. John's, begun to learn how to manage his own time.

After supplying himself with a thirty-six-month calendar, Don used part of that first year to schedule meetings with a variety of groups at First Church. During the first six months Don and Mary had attended three dozen "cottage meetings" at which volunteers in the church had hosted a series of "get acquainted with Don and Mary" evenings in private homes. The attendance at these two-hour events ranged from eight to thirty. That schedule enabled a combined total of 483 different members from First Church to meet Mary and Don in an informal meeting at a total investment of less than one hundred hours of ministerial time.

Another part of that self-imposed discipline of spending more time with groups of people was Don's schedule of meeting twice a year with the officers from the chancel choir. This meeting came a few days after John Owen had submitted his resignation, but three weeks remained before his departure from the scene.

Staffing the Ministry of Music

"I agree, the time has come for us to have a full-time minister of music," declared one of the two tenors from the choir. "Now that John has announced his resignation, we need to move from a part-time choir director to a full-time person."

"A couple of choir members have warned me this would be on the agenda tonight," replied Don, "so I'm not surprised. Now, tell me why you think we need to replace John with a full-time minister of music?"

"Well, first of all, the choir's been getting the short end of the stick around here for years," bellowed the only bass among the officers. "I joined this choir sixteen years ago, and we never have received the support we deserve. I think we have some things coming to us, and one of them is a full-time choir director. I have absolutely no complaints about John, he's done a superb job! John's given himself and his gifts far beyond what we have any right to expect for what we've been paying him, but I agree the time has come to bring in a professionally trained full-time minister of music!"

"Yes, we need someone who will have the time to develop a full-scale program," chimed in another long-time choir member. "John has been a wonderful director for us in the chancel choir, but we need someone with the training and experience who can build a much larger music program."

* * *

This conversation introduces a few of the dynamics at work in what may be the most complicated area of programming facing leaders of the large church. It also raises the question of how to staff the ministry of music. At least a half dozen approaches can be identified, each substantially different from the others in terms of assumptions and expectations, but with considerable overlap on the surface in terms of what appears to be a table of organization.

The one that appears to be the goal of many active participants in the ministry of music in the large churches, especially in the southeastern states, is to add a full-time professionally trained minister of music to the staff. In some cases one of the most obvious motivations, as the bass made clear to Pastor Johnson, is, "We deserve it!" Providing for a full-time minister of music is a means of recognizing the value of the chancel choir. In simple political terms the choir deserves a piece of patronage when the political spoils are being divided. (The classic definition of a political decision is the allocation of scarce resources among competing demands.)

An overlapping, and usually a far more openly discussed, motivation is to move from an emphasis on one "big choir" and several "little choirs" to a more comprehensive music program with a variety of components. The usual assumption accompanying this demand, which also was articulated very clearly to Pastor Johnson, was that only a full-time and professionally trained person can produce that result.

This approach often leads to (a) a search for a dynamic and creative minister of music who can and will produce that comprehensive music program and (b) disappointment since it is only the very rare person who can do that single-handedly. This approach also assumes that one person can relate to a variety of volunteers effectively, enlist them, inspire them, organize them, motivate them, direct them, and also win a positive response from all of them. In many cases this approach is more than simply a search for a professionally trained minister of music; it is a search for a middle-sized miracle!

A second, more realistic, and far more sophisticated approach is to seek a full-time minister of music who, instead of setting out single-handedly to build a comprehensive music program, is asked to join the staff and cause that to happen.

The easiest way to distinguish between these two approaches is to listen in on the budget discussions. When the first approach is being discussed, the focus is on how much additional money will be required for the compensation package for a full-time choir director. When the second approach is being discussed, the discussion is on the total budget for a full-scale music program, including the salaries of several part-time directors, the purchase of additional sheet music, supplies, organ maintenance, piano tuning, and a half dozen other items.

This second approach is based on the assumption that it is unrealistic to expect one person to possess all the skills necessary to do everything or to relate effectively to all age groups, that the size of the task requires more than 2,500 hours a year, and that there is a huge difference between "doing it" and "causing it to happen."

This second approach calls for finding a minister of music who possesses superior skills in (a) enlisting and training a staff of volunteers and/or part-time paid choir directors, (b) building and nurturing large groups, and (c) building the staff necessary to create an extensive and varied music program.[1]

A third approach is by far the most common and typically includes a part-time director for the chancel choir who also may direct one or two other choirs, plus a couple of other persons, who may or may not be paid, who direct a children's choir or two, a handbell choir and perhaps the youth choir plus the part-time organist. This is the frugal approach that often is resented by some choir members who believe it symbolizes the low value placed on music by that congregation. To be more precise, it may be an appropriate approach for the thousands of congregations averaging a hundred to three hundred people at Sunday morning worship who are reasonably comfortable on that plateau in size and have no serious ambitions to grow in numbers. At best it is only an interim or transitional approach for larger congregations seeking to challenge the members in their spiritual journeys, expecting to reach and serve a growing number of people and/or attempting to use the power of music as one of the foundation stones in the total ministry, program, and outreach of that church.

A fourth, not uncommon, and clearly the worst approach to staffing the ministry of music is based on the assumption that adversarial relationships can be productive within the life of the worshiping community.[2] This approach sees the total program of that congregation as a series of highly competitive fiefdoms. If the Christian education committee is successful in securing the funds to hire a children's worker, then "by golly, since they got theirs, next year we're entitled to ours." Whenever a competing program area is able to expand its staff, equal treatment demands that every other program department should be allocated the resources necessary to expand its staff. Empire building and competition, rather than ministry and outreach, become the key criteria for the allocation of scarce resources. This approach may be innocently encouraged by a long-range planning committee's report that prescribes, on a year-by-year schedule, how the total staff will be enlarged. What is a means-to-an-end paragraph in their report is translated into a report card on how various program areas have been graded in what is perceived to be a competition for resources. The "winner" is recommended to be the recipient of additional resources in the first year of that five-year plan and the "loser" either is on the list for the fifth year, or even worse, does not even make the list. (This response to an innocent recommendation illustrates the doctrine of original sin or the power of egocentricity or both.)

A fifth, and perhaps the rarest approach to staffing the ministry of music, is to concentrate on the larger context that first of all this is a community of believers who have come together to worship God and to proclaim Jesus Christ as Lord and Savior in all the world. Therefore the primary organizing principle in creating any type of music troup is that it be a religious community. The chancel choir is first of all a caring, praying, loving, mutually supportive, religious community and second it is a vocal group organized to sing praises to God. Every handbell choir is first of all a religious community. The youth choir is first of all a religious community designed to help teenagers grow in the faith and second it is a vocal group.

To implement this approach the search committee looks first for someone who displays an open and strong relationship with a living Lord, who is skilled and comfortable in articulating his or her faith as a Christian, who feels compelled to share that faith with others, and who makes very clear that Christ is far more important than music in his or her life. Ideally that person also will have a track record of having been able to create meaningful religious communities in one or more other churches. The large congregation often is able to expect skills that have been put into practice elsewhere and gifts that have been utilized in other settings.

A second characteristic of the person who follows this

approach to the ministry of music is a clear and unreserved conviction that the primary audience for that anthem is God, not the people in the pews.

Third, the search committee seeking a musician with this approach will look for someone who is able to (a) create a religious community out of people who want to be part of the chancel choir, (b) help that chancel choir model this concept for other groups in the music program, (c) enlist other leaders, either paid or volunteer, who can create religious communities as they organize and direct a youth choir or a handbell choir or a flute choir or an orchestra or a children's choir or a drama group or a liturgical dance team (that often is the easiest group to organize as a religious community), (d) conceptualize and build an extensive music program and (e) feel comfortable being the leader in only one of several religious communities in that congregation rather than being *the* leader of every component of this program.

It should go without saying that an essential foundation for this approach is a senior minister who fully comprehends and whole-heartedly supports this approach, who is a secure individual personally, professionally, emotionally, and spiritually, who is content to be one of the spiritual leaders of that congregation rather than demanding the role as *the* spiritual leader, and who comprehends how music can be a powerful force in the faith journey.

A sixth approach to staffing the ministry of music begins with a radically different basic assumption. Instead of assuming that the primary focus is on worship and music, this approach begins by looking at the congregation and at the needs of the members.

This may be the appropriate approach for the long-established, large, and diverse congregation that in fact is a federation of generations of members. One generation of today's members may be composed of the people who were attracted by Dr. Doyle when he was the senior minister here, a slightly younger generation joined back when this congregation had the biggest and best Sunday school in the city, a third generation joined under the leadership of the Reverend Griffin, a fourth generation can be traced back to when this congregation first developed a strong Bible study program under the Reverend Reese, and a fifth generation joined since the arrival of the present senior minister. The outsider looking in is reminded of the several strata of rock and earth out where the highway department recently made the cut through the hill for a new road.

Each generation of members joined to have a particular set of religious needs met and those religious needs were met at that time. The long-tenured members are now at a different stage of their spiritual and life journeys. They came for one reason. They remain because of a combination of several factors including habit, inertia, comfort, friendship ties, investment, and fear of the unknown. Together the old and the new represent a highly diverse collection of people. One member greets the pastor at the door following worship with, "That was one of the two or three best sermons I've heard in the thirty-seven years I've been a member here!" The next person in line, overhearing those words, feels pressured to be both complimentary, but also honest, and the only phrase he or she can think of that meets both criteria is, "Good morning, Pastor."

Several are convinced the organ is too loud, while others believe the organist plays too rapidly and a few want a faster pace. Thirty were convinced the selection of the opening hymn that day was an inspired choice, twenty hate it passionately, and four hundred cannot recall what it was.

That congregation may include 135 persons who could be members of the chancel choir, 53 are carried on the roster of that choir, 29 rarely miss, 16 informally take turns staying away, and 8 will return after the present choir director is replaced, which they hope will be day after tomorrow, while 27 pray that day is at least twenty years away. Out of the remaining 82 potential members of the chancel choir, 23 have not volunteered because they see themselves as good, but not sufficiently gifted for what they are convinced is really a major league choir. Another 14 would be in that chancel choir, except they are convinced they are not needed. Somewhere between 10 and 15 have excellent voices but are too lazy to make it to rehearsal. Another half dozen are waiting for someone to personally beg them to join. Perhaps a dozen, more or less, would join, except the choir rehearses on

Thursday evening and they have other urgent commitments for that evening. An overlapping group of 20 to 30 members could be valuable members of that chancel choir but they are repelled by (a) most of the anthems the choir sings or (b) the choir director or (c) both of the above. A final overlapping group of 25 or 30 out of those 82 potential members offer as the primary reason for their absence, "The choir sings at eleven o'clock and we always come to the first service."

In this setting the appropriate approach for staffing the ministry of music is built around the concept of redundancy. The operational assumption is that no matter what course of action is chosen, some people will be opposed; no matter what anthem is selected, at least a few will condemn it as a dumb decision; no matter what the central organizing principle is for creating a new music group, some people will stay away; and no matter who directs the youth choir, at least one-third to one-half of the teenagers will boycott it.

Instead of seeking a personable and talented musician who will build the program, this approach begins by defining the components of the total program. This approach can be summarized by a series of statements that might read something like these.

We need to organize a choir for the eleven o'clock service, with a director who can make people sing better than they know how to sing. We need to organize a choir for the early service that first of all is a model of a religious community (who else will come to sing at eight o'clock in the morning?) and second can be an enjoyable learning experience for those who believe they are not sufficiently talented for the chancel choir. They might rehearse at eleven o'clock so we can include the people who cannot come to the Thursday evening rehearsal. We need an adult choir at the middle-hour service that can be an entry point for young adults into our church, and we need someone to direct it who displays the winsome personality necessary to attract young adults.

We need someone who can build a liturgical dance team around the combination of this as (a) a means of praising God, (b) an opportunity to express your commitment both to God and to this church, (c) a chance to express your creativity through a non-verbal channel, (d) a possibility for expanding the group life of this congregation by creating another mutual support group organized around witness, creativity, service, and learning, and (e) a means of facilitating the assimilation of new members.

We need someone who can organize a youth choir around the combination of excellence in vocal music, service, trips, perfecting a new skill, discipline, and high expectations. Since we can expect that two-thirds of our high school youth will not respond to this, we need someone else who can organize a youth handbell choir with the goal of at least one-half male participation. We need a completely different personality who can organize a group of teenagers who have zero interest in music, who are not part of any mutual support group in their high school, who may be experiencing a troubled home life, and who need help in surviving adolescence. We also need someone who can organize and lead what at least some teenagers will find to be a meaningful Bible study group that will help them in their journey of faith. We need someone who can organize a collection of seven to fifteen teenagers around the themes of service, sacrifice, and study and for that we need a person, or better yet, a team of adult volunteers, who also model the role of an adult Christian.

Where can you find a minister of music who is able and willing to accept the responsibility for a program defined in those terms? (A full statement of this approach would require parallel paragraphs in drama, Sunday school, children's ministries, and large group events.) The probable answer is: You will not be able to find a minister of music who is comfortable with this approach.

This sixth approach is appropriate only in those large and heterogeneous congregations that have decided that a key component of their response to diversity is to subordinate the traditional categories of music, youth, children's ministries, Sunday school, fellowship, and the assimilation of new members under the broad umbrella of program. In perhaps one-fourth of one percent of all large churches utilizing this approach, the program director also directs the chancel choir. That is a coincidence, not a requirement for this approach.

Instead of asking one person to be responsible for a music program, this approach expects the program director to be responsible for all programming, including music. Typically, this means the program director works with other paid program specialists, many of whom will be part-time, plus a large cadre of volunteers, some of whom serve as part of a team such as team teaching in the Sunday school or the team that works with a youth group or the team responsible for the music encounter program for young children or the team that is in charge of the Wednesday after-school youth club.

A seventh approach overlaps two or three of these, but its central organizing principles include: (1) learning, perfecting, and practicing a new skill can be a powerful organizing concept, (2) the minister of music not only is a superb teacher, but also is highly competent at enlisting and training teachers, and (3) every music group is built around learning and practicing skills in music. The music program resembles a large school with the minister of music serving as the principal.

Which of these approaches comes closest to fitting the personality and needs of your congregation? Or do you need to follow a different approach in staffing your ministry of music? Are you more comfortable with music as a separate program area? Or do you prefer that vocal choirs be seen as components of a larger program? How do you conceptualize the place of music in building a program staff? How you staff may determine the relationship of music groups to the total program.

Creative Artist or Staff Member?

"Tell me how you persuaded your choir director to resign," the senior minister of a nearby large church asked Don Johnson as these two new friends were having lunch together. "I inherited a full-time minister of music I'm ready to see move on. He's a great musician and an excellent choir director, but he also is the least cooperative member of our staff. In the three years I've been here I doubt if he has been on time more than twice for our weekly staff meeting, and he's missed at least two dozen when I know he's been in town.

It's almost impossible to get him to cooperate with me on anything. Last Sunday, for example, I was preaching a sermon on salvation built around Jesus as Savior and he had the choir rehearsed to sing an anthem on God the creator. My predecessor allowed him to choose the hymns, and it took me six months to get back the right to choose the hymns I wanted to go with my sermon. When I talk to him, I sometimes get the feeling that he is on another planet in another solar system in some faraway galaxy!"

"Sounds as if you have a real problem," sympathized Don. This senior minister does have a problem. It is a problem faced by a huge number of senior ministers. It also is a problem troubling the life of perhaps an even larger number of ministers of music.

What Is the Problem?

On the surface it appears to be a problem of incompatible personalities or a difference of opinion over goals or a refusal by the minister of music to recognize and accept his or her place on the local deference pyramid or a lack of self-discipline on the part of the minister of music or a conflict over priorities or fundamental differences about the nature and meaning of corporate worship.

That may be an overly simplistic diagnosis of the situation. Another approach to understanding this point of conflict can be introduced by looking at two different worlds. The first clue to understanding the differences between these two worlds is to picture in your mind a group of children out playing on a sunny Tuesday afternoon in early May. As one watches these children at play words and phrases such as those in the left-hand column in the box on the next page may be used to describe that scene.

Now, change the subject and picture in your mind that weekly staff meeting of a large congregation one morning in May. As you peek through a crack in the partially open door, the words in the right-hand column of the box on the next page may come to your mind as you silently watch that staff meeting for thirty or forty minutes. As you compare the two lists, you may want to ask yourself where you would prefer to

Children at Play	*Staff Meeting*
Rhythm	Verbal
Joy	Orderly
Movement	Schedules
Creativity	Planning
Laughter	Calendars
Imagination	Reports
Spontaneity	Frowns
Emotions	Rational
Noise	Abstract
Disorder	Tensions
Relationships	Smiles
Intuitive	Hierarchy
Tenderness	Sit
Change of pace	Watch
Timelessness	Listen
Rituals	Study
Uninhibited	Passivity
Experiences	Punctual
Sounds	Agenda
Color	Frustrations
Play	Talk
Visual	Boredom
Relaxed	Piety
	Conflict

spend the next two hours, watching the children play or participating in that staff meeting?

A second clue can be seen by looking at the snow fall one overcast day in February. The photographer looks out and sees the opportunity to take some black and white photographs that will be filled with shadows, silhouettes, and contrasts. Others watch the snow fall and worry about highway accidents, delays in airline flights, extra work, or being late to a meeting.

A third clue is in the system used to evaluate employees. In one the criteria for setting the rewards are creativity, innovation, new ideas, productivity, and imagination. In another organization the evaluation procedures reward punctuality, neatness, productivity, skills in interpersonal relationships, competence, cooperation around attaining common goals, and conformity with the organizational culture.

The first world described in each of these three examples is the one that nurtures the creative artist. The second is the world inhabited by that far larger number of people who have learned how to function reasonably effectively and comfortably in a complex institutional setting. The first is a world inhabited largely by free-spirited individuals. The second is a culture that emphasizes groups, teams, and hierarchies.

The best and the most effective ministries of music come from the world of the creative artist. That world has a different reward system, uses a different language, and creates a different institutional culture than the world that produces most of the staff members for the large congregation. This comparison is further complicated by the fact that a relatively small number of ministers of music, and a few other staff members, have mastered the necessary skills to fit comfortably into both worlds. They provide a comparison base that causes the vast majority of people to feel inadequate and to be perceived as inadequate. Technically that can be defined as an unfair labor practice.

It may help in defining this distinction to remember that while it is the great football teams that win the Super Bowl, most great paintings were created by one person and few great sculptures were carved by a committee. Creative artists tend to be individuals.

The most effective and respected senior ministers have learned how to live and function in that second world, and they expect all staff members, with the possible exception of the financial secretary or computer operator, to be comfortable with the culture and expectations of that second world. Typically these senior ministers can appreciate the gifts of the creative artist, but they also seek conformity and a willingness to migrate to that second world. Some creative artists are willing, as a price of their freedom, to visit that second world for a few hours every week for staff meetings and other occasions, but many cannot see the need or value of even those occasional visits. A few grew up in that second world, escaped from it many years ago, and simply cannot bear to return to it. Others, it appears, fear the culture of that second world may be contagious and conclude the safest course is to avoid any possible contamination.

The wise senior minister (a) understands the existence of these radically different worlds, (b) recognizes and affirms the native habitat of the creative artist, (c) sees the conflict in perspective, culture, and values between these two worlds as a natural phenomenon, not as a product of personalities, (d) is reasonably comfortable with the fact this means trade-offs and is willing to work at making those trade-offs reasonably free of severe pain, (e) does not expect or require everyone to move into and operate from a base in that second world, (f) values the creative stimulation that can be produced by visits by people from one world to the other, (g) does not project identical expectations of people regardless of the world they live in, and (h) accepts the fact that living with ambiguity is one of the price tags for being a happy, effective, and healthy senior pastor.

As he reflected on the best approach to staffing the ministry of music at First Church, Pastor Don Johnson eventually had to deal with the existence of these two worlds. What he could not overlook, however, even for a brief period of time, is the fact that the larger the congregation, the greater the power and importance of music.

The Power of Music

For centuries the leaders of armies, those responsible for planning a huge parade or the persons responsible for a big evangelistic rally have understood the power of music with crowds of people. Music can bring unity out of chaos, music can inspire, music can motivate, music can create a feeling of cohesiveness and music can move people emotionally.

A common error in large congregations is to underestimate the power of music. This can be illustrated by those congregations that change the Sunday morning schedule from one to two worship experiences but do not organize a choir for that first early service. It can be seen in the efforts of those efficiency-oriented individuals who seek to eliminate that opening hymn from the weekly gathering of that huge adult Sundy school on the grounds that will leave more time for the lesson. Equally questionable is the decision in the large church to turn to the music budget as a place to achieve saving when the time has come to cut the proposed budget.

One of the battles Don Johnson encountered at First Church was to gain a substantial increase in the funds for the budget of the music program. The argument he faced was, "After we begin to see a substantial increase in our attendance, that will be the time to expand the music budget." Don's response was that an expansion of the music program was a critical component of any strategy to increase attendance.

Pastor Johnson contended that First Church should see itself, not as a congregation of eight hundred plus members, but as a congregation of congregations, classes, groups, cells, choirs, circles, fellowships, organizations, and clubs. That was one of the arguments he used in his campaign to return to the schedule of the early 1960s at First Church, which included two worship services on Sunday morning.

Unlike smaller congregations that frequently project a self-image of "one big family," First Church, Don felt, needed the expansion of the structured and organized group life to reach and include more people. First Church was far too large for most people to gain a sense of belonging by simply taking the vows of membership. Larger churches must respond to this need for inclusion by functioning as a collection or federation of subgroups. The various choirs are essential contributors to the group life of the larger congregations. In many churches, for example, a list of the three or four most closely knit and cohesive groups out of the many subgroups in that congregation often will include perhaps one or two adult Sunday school classes, the adult choir, and a circle in the women's organization that has been together for years. The larger the congregation, the more important the contributions of the music program to the group life. The church of two or three hundred members may have only two or three choirs, while the one-thousand-member parish should include seven to ten choirs and other musical groups.

A second reason why the music program is a unique and valuable asset in the large churches grows out of the "admission requirements" for the choir. Many of the various subgroups in most churches are for couples while others are for parents or women or families or youth or persons with administrative gifts. The basic requirement for admission into the choir is an interest in, and it is hoped, some talent for vocal music. As a result the choir often is one of the few places where the single adult, and especially the bachelor, can participate and be included without some reference to that person's marital status. In a majority of churches the choir is the one group in that congregation where the single adult can feel welcome, needed, and appreciated. For some singles it is their only entry point into an active participatory role in that congregation.

At this point it also should be noted that most Christian churches have far more entry points for women than for men. This can be seen in the Sunday school and in the vocal choirs. Typically two-thirds of the regular participants in the adult choir are women, many of whom also combine the roles of homemaker, mother, and wife with a full-time job. One of the values of an instrumental group is that it is far more likely than a vocal choir to have a male majority. Those who are concerned about the disappearance of men from the church should not underestimate the attractiveness to men of a brass ensemble or of an orchestra.

The degree of anonymity increases as the size of the congregation increases and this is especially true as adults look at children and youth. They tend to receive very little direct attention from most of the members. Many teenagers, however, possess talents and skills in vocal music that exceed those of most adults and a strong ministry of music enables many young persons to feel they are on the "giving" end of ministry, rather than on the "receiving" end as a result of the largesses of the adults. Active youth participation in the ministry of music changes the role of the teenagers from anonymous recipients of ministry to highly visible, respected, and admired contributors to the total ministry of that congregation.

A fourth, but less universal value of the ministry of music—and one that often is overlooked—can be seen in those congregations that either broadcast the worship service over the radio or televise the Sunday morning worship experience. For the listeners and viewers the music is an essential element of that worship experience. Perhaps the best evidence of this can be found in those congregations that broadcast only 28 or 29 minutes of their hour-long Sunday morning worship service. The listeners complain more about the omission of the anthem by the choir than about the deletion of the pastoral prayer or the omission of the reading from the Scriptures. When the constraints of the radio or TV time period force choices, the two sacred and untouchable components of that half-hour broadcast are the sermon and the anthem!

Another dimension of the music program that often is overlooked expands an earlier point. This is the ministry with youth. This is a sensitive issue, the subject of tremendous anxiety in most large churches, and one part of a subsequent chapter. The two most widely followed approaches to developing a large youth group are (a) build it around the magnetic personality of the youth director or youth minister who attracts teenagers in a manner similar to an outdoor electric light attracting moths on a summer evening or (b) build it around a youth choir or around a youth-music-drama focal point. While many church leaders have well-earned reservations about the first approach, the second is one that deserves serious attention. It is both effective and good. It is an especially attractive concept in those large churches that offer two or three or more different opportunities for meaningful involvement by teenagers.

A sixth reason why music can be a valuable asset in the large church grows out of the fact that it is rare in the big congregations for every person present for corporate worship to know everyone else. How can a collection of strangers, visitors, and casual acquaintances be turned into a worshiping community?

This usually is not a problem in the small church where everyone knows one another and many are related to several other members. This depersonalization of anonymity is an important consideration in the large congregation and one of the most practical responses is congregational singing. When people sing together, the inevitable result is a sense of friendliness, unity, and cohesiveness. Older readers can remember this from the "sing alongs" with the bouncing ball at the movies in the pre-television era. Veterans of military service can recall this effect from their days as recruits. Football fans can recognize this dynamic from attending college and university football games. The choir that can lead and encourage widespread congregational singing is a tremendous asset in the large church. Music and strong congregational singing can make the stranger feel an integral part of that worshiping community within minutes after walking through the door.

Finally, and perhaps most important, is the issue of how we express our faith as Christians. Through the centuries Christians have used many different channels to express their faith. These include preaching, baptism, personal witnessing, tithing, participation in corporate worship, sharing in the Lord's Supper, martyrdom, the construction of cathedrals, teaching, constructing and operating hospitals and homes for those in need, sculpture, painting, sending missionaries to every corner of the world, fasting, writing, organizing new congregations, visiting those in jail, creating educational institutions such as Harvard, Yale, or nursery schools for three-year-olds, providing chaplains for a variety of institutions, care of the widowed, maintenance of cemeteries, and music. Through the centuries music has been one of the most important channels for expressing the Christian faith. Martin Luther, Charles Wesley, Johann Sebastian Bach, Ludwig von Beethoven, and Isaac Watts are but five of many names that could be cited to illustrate the importance of music in expressing the Christian faith.

In general, the larger the congregation the more important it is to utilize several different channels in expressing the Christian faith. Or, in other words, the larger the membership, the more important music becomes as a channel for expressing and communicating the faith.

That is why expanding the music program was so high on Don Johnson's list of priorities at First Church.

Buildings, Money,
and Self-Esteem

Chapter Four

Although he clearly had mixed feelings about making a means-to-end issue a high priority in his first years at First Church, Pastor Don Johnson soon was able to talk himself into making the renovation of the fellowship hall and the expansion of the parking lot the top priority for the governing board.

Don pointed out to the Board the possibility of a once-in-a-lifetime opportunity to acquire additional land and the deteriorating condition of the fellowship hall. When the trustees suggested a modest renovation of the fellowship hall, Don asked the Board to appoint a special study committee to look at the overall needs. That committee was not appointed until May of Don's first year and did not report until the following October. They had been able to secure a thirty-day option to purchase the store and lot adjacent to the parking lot owned by First Church. This study also recommended a complete renovation of the fellowship hall at an estimated cost of $800,000. The option price on the store and lot was $285,000.

When this report came to the Board, a few members were stunned into silence, a couple nodded glum approval, and several began to question whether a congregation this small could afford to spend over a million dollars on real estate. Some argued that was an impossible goal; others contended that money could better be spent on missions, but at least four or five were ready to start a fund-raising campaign that evening. After nearly two hours of discussion, it was agreed to place this report at the top of the agenda for the November meeting. A month later the first person to speak, a good friend and strong ally of the senior minister, moved that a special action committee be appointed with authority to prepare a plan for a capital funds appeal. This seemed to be a good way to get a complex item off the Board's agenda and was seconded and approved within ten minutes. At the January meeting this special action committee asked for the Board's approval to go ahead with a "Miracle Sunday" plan to raise $1,050,000 on the second Sunday in May, five weeks before the scheduled celebration of the 105th anniversary of the founding of First Church. The odd amount was explained as $10,000 times the age of this congregation and also approximately equal to the anticipated expenditures.

The Board approved the plan and gave permission for this special action committee to go ahead, but three-quarters of the members remained convinced the goal was unattainable.

During the twelve weeks before Mother's Day the action committee called on slightly more than eighty of the members they believed would be among the most generous supporters and also initiated a multi-faceted effort to acquaint the members with the need. This campaign included (a) pictures of dead rats Virgil had found in the fellowship hall, (b) a line drawing of the expanded parking lot, (c) an architect's rendering of the appearance of the building after the removal of the store (the trustees had negotiated the purchase of that property with a one-year bank loan), (d) a series of one-minute speeches every Sunday morning for ten weeks, (e) hour-long visits to every adult group, class, choir, committee, and organization at First Church, (f) two "public hearing" meetings to answer questions, and (g) a series of seven first-class letters to all member households plus three dozen constituent families.

The first of these seven letters explained the need and came from the widely respected and influential layman who chaired this special action committee. The second letter came from a widely respected and influential laywoman who elaborated on the need and the urgency. The third letter came from Don and was primarily a stewardship plea. The fourth letter came from the person who chaired the Board and was an inspirational "let's all get behind this and make it happen for the extension of God's kingdom" appeal.

By the time the date had rolled around to prepare the fifth letter, which was written by a third member of this special action committee, enthusiasm had begun to build. The heart of this fifth letter asked, "How much is $1,050,000?" The answer was: "To meet that goal we will need at least two gifts of $100,000 or more, four of $50,000 or more, eight of $25,000 or more, ten of $10,000 or more, twenty of $5,000 or more plus hundreds more in the $5 to $5,000 bracket." This aroused three or four complaints, "You're saying my contribution of $50 is not worth giving, but that's all I can afford." The answer, of course, was it would take 21,000 fifty dollar contributions from what by now had grown to be a 932-member congregation to produce $1,050,000, but everyone was too polite to mention that. The protesters were told in a sympathetic voice, "Every dollar will help us reach our goal."

Those earlier visits made it possible for the person who chaired this effort to write a letter that arrived twelve days before Mother's Day. It began, "As you all know, our goal is to raise in a special one day offering $1,050,000. Some of you have told me you would be delighted if we raised a half million dollars. Others have said we'll be lucky if we get $300,000. Well, friends, Miracle Sunday is still twelve days away and we already have received $373,527! If we all get behind this and support it, your committee is convinced our congregation can meet this challenge, but we need your generous support to reach that target." A few more paragraphs elaborated on the need and urged people to give this prayerful consideration before making a final decision on the amount of their contribution. The last paragraph invited everyone to stay for a carry-in lunch after worship on Mother's Day.

Each letter was on personal-sized stationery with the name and address of the sender at the very top followed by the name and address of the recipient and a personal salutation. Each came in an envelope with the sender's name and address typed in the upper-left corner and the recipient's name and address typed, no labels. The office computer did all of that. Each letter was personally signed in colored ink by the sender and about a fourth included a personalized postscript at the bottom of the three-sheet letter. Every letter carried a first-class colorful commemorative stamp. All letters were mailed with the hope they would arrive on Tuesday, the day when the quantity of first-class mail received is the lowest of the week for many people. The total cost for stationery, envelopes, and postage was a little under $1,000, but this effort did tie up the office computer and printer for many hours and the action committee plus some volunteers spent four evenings stuffing and stamping envelopes.

Everyone who wanted to and could remained for lunch after worship on Mother's Day. A little before one o'clock three happy members of the committee came in to announce the total amount contributed was $1,183,781. This was greeted by a moment of stunned silence followed by thunderous applause.

The following Wednesday, the seventh letter, personally signed by every member of this special action committee including the senior minister, was mailed. It thanked everyone for their generous support, announced that the final total was $1,194,369, and concluded with a paragraph asking God's guidance on the next steps.

On Friday afternoon a man who lived alone and was widely perceived as an inactive member and who had not contributed to this appeal, stopped by the office and left a check for $56,000 with Lillian with the comment, "Tell Pastor Johnson it'll be easier to remember the amount if we round it off at a little over a quarter of a million dollars." When Don stopped by his house that evening to thank him, the man was not at home, but he was in church nearly every Sunday for the next several years and subsequently became one of Don Johnson's best friends and most aggressive supporters.

It also was of interest to Don to discover that three of the seven largest contributors to this special appeal were not from among the eighty households which the members of this special action committee earlier had identified as the people most likely to be generous contributors. Two of these three and four of the top ten contributors were widowed women.

For the second time in two years the June meeting of the Board convened with everyone present. The other time had been Don's first meeting. After thanking the special capital funds committee for their amazing success and enjoying a half dozen stories about relatively unknown dimensions of this effort, the Board agreed with Don's suggestion that the person chairing the Board be asked to bring to the July meeting a list of nominees to staff a new action committee that would accept responsibility for the renovation of the fellowship hall, the demolition of the store, and the expansion of the parking lot. The closest to a dissent came from one member who remarked, "I'm still in shock at the idea of paying $10,000 for each additional parking space, but I guess we can afford it. It might have been cheaper to buy thirty cars from our members who live nearby on condition they always walk to church."

Two years later, a couple of months before the 107th anniversary celebration, the renovated and expanded fellowship hall was in use.

Was That a Wise Step?

As Don Johnson repeatedly reflected on his earlier decision to make this such a high priority, he gradually built up an extensive rationale for that course of action. His list included these seven reasons.

1. Additional off-street parking was an absolute necessity, especially for weekday and evening programs, and this was an opportunity that might not come again for years. As it turned out, that store and its parking lot was the only property in the block that came on the market during Don's entire tenure at First Church.

2. Although it is true the fellowship hall is a tool of ministry, and a means-to-an-end, it was a worn-out tool. The renovation was badly overdue.

3. The congregation as a whole had drifted into a state of passivity during Dr. Bennington's last years. One way of

breaking that passivity was a specific, challenging, attainable, easily measurable, highly visible, and unifying goal that required widespread support and could be an important rallying point. The building program provided that goal. The unfortunate part of the choice was that it soon was completed and thus became yesterday's rallying point.

4. Overlapping that was Don's conviction that the concept of momentum applies to churches as well as to football teams and political parties. Newton's first law of motion explains that a body in motion will tend to stay in motion and a body at rest will tend to remain at rest, unless acted upon by some outside force. Pastor Don Johnson saw the combination of the capital funds appeal, the renovation and expansion of the fellowship hall and the acquisition of additional land as that outside force needed to get First Church back in motion. Once in motion the momentum would make it easier to accomplish other goals.

5. Perhaps most critical was the need to respond to the low level of self-esteem that pervaded the atmosphere at First Church. The last significant congregational victory had been the restoration, following the fire of 1967. Well over two-thirds of the current membership had joined since the completion of that venture. The success of Miracle Sunday was the challenge to climb a mountain beyond the capability of this congregation. When that perceived-as-unattainable goal was surpassed, many concluded, "If we can do that we can tackle anything!" This victory raised the level of self-esteem. That victory also was a foundation on which to build other changes including subsequent efforts to expand the financial base.

6. As he began to discover how the general community perceived First Church, this new senior minister recognized the need to renew the community image. Don discovered the widespread feeling was "First Church has been on the decline ever since Dr. Doyle left nearly a quarter of a century ago." While that was not completely accurate, it was a widely shared view. The expansion of the parking lot and the renovation of the fellowship hall would help the rest of the community see that the people at First Church were sure, "Our best days are still ahead of us and we're getting

ready for them." Miracle Sunday, of course, was perceived by outsiders as a miracle.

7. Finally, Don accepted the fact that while he had been officially installed as the new senior minister, he had to earn the role of leader. This was a part of that process of earning the right to be accepted as "our leader." Don did not possess the magnetic personality that attracted followers. Unlike grace, which is a gift, leadership frequently has to be earned.

Anyone reading this seven-point list also should realize that Don Johnson, like most other competent leaders, could talk himself into what he wanted to believe. Don wanted to erase all doubts, either in his own mind or in anyone else's head, that this had been a worthwhile venture. These seven arguments helped him accomplish that and he used them repeatedly.

Broadening the Financial Base

While the level of giving was well above average when compared to denomination-wide averages, during Dr. Bennington's last years, it really was only average when examined in the light of needs and potential or when compared to other large and numerically growing churches.

As part of his overall strategy for change, Pastor Johnson was able to persuade the leaders at First Church to broaden their thinking. For decades they had been taught four lessons by a succession of pastors. First, contributions to the church come out of members' current income. (This is a widely followed concept that became obsolete during the 1960s.) Second, the best approach is to rely on a unified budget and reduce the number of special appeals. Third, except for certain youth efforts, all money-raising activities should be forbidden. Fourth, expenditures should be kept within the limits of projected income.

The easiest change came with the success of Miracle Sunday. After that, the leaders saw the need and approved the concept of asking people to contribute out of *both* current income and accumulated wealth. The lifting of the ban on money-raising activities is described in the next chapter. The increase in the number of special appeals was a long battle and was won on the pragmatic grounds that it was the only way to expand benevolence giving without inhibiting program expansion. The success of Miracle Sunday and the resulting improvement in the level of self-esteem plus the growth in numbers made it fairly easy to convert the leaders to the concept that expenditures should be determined by needs rather than by last year's level of income, but that was a seven-year battle.

In addition, Don helped the leaders see the need for encouraging (a) more bequests, (b) a greater emphasis on special needs that could be funded with memorial gifts, (c) more reliance on user fees, and (d) positive choices offered people through special appeals. The increase in the emphasis on bequests was not difficult since First Church already had a substantial endowment fund from earlier bequests. The trustees also supported this when it was decided that income from the endowment fund would be used to match member giving on a dollar-for-dollar basis for that separate mainte- nance fund. The endowment fund already had its own separate set of trustees, none of whom could hold any other policy-making office while serving as a trustee of that endowment fund. They preferred the income from the endowment fund be restricted entirely for missions and scholarships, but reluctantly agreed to that change.

From a long-term perspective one of the biggest changes Don brought to First Church was the suggestion to create a separate legal corporation called the Twenty-First Century Foundation. This corporation, with a set of seven trustees elected from among the members of First Church, raised and disbursed funds solely for local missions and outreach. By the end of Don's sixth year it was disbursing almost $250,000 a year to a variety of social welfare and social justice causes, several of which had been initiated by trustees of that foundation. This enabled First Church (a) to avoid some diversionary and divisive battles by keeping these items out of the regular budget and off the agenda of the annual meeting, (b) to raise more money for these causes than would have been possible through the regular budgeting process, (c) to attract and assimilate a number of new members who admired this concept and wanted to be a part of making it work, (d) to gain credibility where previously that credibility had been lacking, and (e) to respond quickly to some urgent and unanticipated needs.

From another perspective this emphasis on real estate and financial concerns also freed the agenda in subsequent years so ministry and outreach could dominate the thinking of most leaders including the staff.

The Women's Organization and the Church School

Chapter Five

A few months after Miracle Sunday when it was Anne's turn to preach, she told Don she had an announcement to make before he pronounced the benediction. When the time came, she stepped down out of the pulpit and nodded to a man in a next-to-front row pew who came up to stand beside her. "Friends, I want you to meet Jack Abernathy. Jack and I plan to be married here at First Church the second Saturday in October. You're all invited to come to the wedding."

As one person, the entire congregation rose and applauded for nearly five minutes.

Nearly an hour later, after everyone had finally left, Anne said to Don, "Now you know why I wanted you to pronounce the benediction today. I wasn't sure I could get through it."

"Now I know what the Abernathy wedding on the calendar in the office means," observed Don. "I thought that was a wedding you had scheduled for someone who's not a member here."

"That's correct, Jack's not a member here," agreed Anne. "I've checked your schedule with Mary and Lillian, and they have guaranteed you'll be here and you'll officiate at our wedding."

"You mean both my wife and my secretary knew about this, but you kept it secret from me," challenged Don.

"Yep," replied Anne. "Until today I had told only my very

closest friends, and Mary and Lillian are two of my closest friends."

One of the people who was absolutely delighted to hear this news was Anne's sixty-one-year-old mother. Mrs. Potter had four children, two of whom were married, but Mrs. Potter was still waiting, very impatiently, to become a grandmother. Almost as relieved and delighted was Don Johnson. While he was pleased to learn Anne was planning to get married, and highly impressed with Jack Abernathy, the frosting on the cake came the day after Anne's announcement when she stopped in Don's office and asked, "Want to talk about extending my contract?"

"Sure do," replied Don. "What do you have in mind?"

"Is it okay if I stop looking for my own church and settle in here as your permanent associate minister?" inquired Anne.

"That's a deal," declared Don with genuine enthusiasm, "if that's what you really want. When we promoted you from youth minister a year and a half ago, I told you that I would be delighted if you changed your mind and extended that two-year commitment to twenty years, but do you really want to make this change in your career plans?"

"Let's think in terms of maybe ten years, not twenty," offered Anne, "but there is one reservation. My biological clock is running and I hope I'll need a couple of maternity leaves during these next several years."

"That'll be no problem," declared Don. "Babies make people feel very generous and I know the folks here would much prefer to give you a maternity leave rather than a farewell party. How will all this influence your ministerial career plans?"

"I really don't know," admitted Anne. "I still would like to be the senior minister of a big congregation like this one, but I don't know if that's realistic if I stay here until I'm forty. Is it realistic to think of a woman moving from being an associate minister to becoming the senior pastor of another church?"

The Roads to Becoming a Senior Minister

"Well, a growing number of men have been following that route in recent years," replied Don, "so I don't know why women shouldn't be able to do it. As far as I know, there are at least six or seven roads a person can take to becoming a senior minister. One is to serve for five to twenty years on the staff of a big church and go directly to becoming the senior minister of another large congregation. While that's rare among Methodists, it's increasingly common among Presbyterians, Lutherans, and several other denominations.

"A second road, and perhaps the most heavily traveled, is what I did. First, spend ten or fifteen years in smaller churches and eventually move to becoming the senior minister of a big church. I'm now meeting a lot of senior ministers in their thirties who took a different path. They went out and started a new congregation, helped it grow until more staff was needed, and became a senior minister without moving. Scores of the biggest churches in this country are served by senior ministers who were the founding pastors of those congregations. A parallel road is to go out and become the pastor of a congregation that has the potential for substantial growth, help it grow until the need for more staff is clear, and continue as the senior minister of a multiple-staff church. To some extent that is what happened to me at St. John's. A fifth road is to become the associate pastor and succeed the senior minister when he or she leaves. That's common among Lutherans and Baptists, rare among Methodists, forbidden by Presbyterians, and very common among some of the large independent churches. It also happens in a lot of black and nationality churches.

"A sixth road, which is fairly common among Presbyterians and Baptists, is to go from teaching in a theological seminary to becoming the senior minister of a large church. A similar road is common among Methodists, Baptists, Lutherans, and several smaller denominations and that is to move from a position in the denominational hierarchy to becoming the senior minister of a large church."

"Most of those don't fit me," reflected Anne. "Which do you think is the best?"

"I'm not sure which is the best, but I am sure the worst is the move up the ladder route I've spent the last twenty-five years following," declared Don without hesitation.

"Gee, I'm surprised to hear you say that," said Anne. "I

thought you just said you thought that was the most heavily traveled route."

"I've become convinced it is both the most common route and also the worst," reflected Don. "I've been spending the last five to ten years unlearning almost everything I was taught was the right approach to ministry during my earlier years. I was told a minister should become competent in one-to-one relationships with people. Now that I'm a senior minister, I've had to learn I don't have enough time in the day for that, and I need to become more proficient in working with groups of people. In seminary I was taught the value of small groups and now I see I need better skills in organizing and nurturing large groups. I spent the first fifteen years of my ministry letting other people run my life and reacting to their demands on my day. During the past ten years I've been trying, with limited success, to learn how to manage my time and how to set my own priorities instead of reacting to the expectations of others. I spent nearly fifteen years learning to ask, 'Why?' when someone proposed adding a new program or ministry or group to what I had become convinced was a congregation with limited resources. Now, as a senior minister of a big church with many resources, I'm learning the best response to a proposal for expanding the program or group life is 'Why not?' I spent fifteen years learning that my job as a pastor was to do everything, to be a jack-of-all-trades, and to never offend anyone by saying no. Now I'm trying to learn that my basic responsibility is not to do it, but rather to make sure it gets done. Instead of being a generalist, I'm trying to learn how to be a specialist and how to build a staff of specialists. After spending more than fifteen years learning how to work alone as the only program staff person in the church, I'm still trying to learn how to work as part of a staff team. I spent fifteen years learning to keep the expenditures of the church within the limits of the contributions from the members. If our Miracle Sunday taught us anything, it taught us that's dumb. We should challenge the members to respond to how God has blessed them, not to the limitations of a church budget."

"You're sounding kind of bitter," interrupted Anne.

"No, I'm not bitter," said Don. "I simply realize there is a better road than the one I've taken. Let me give you four more examples. For many years I was taught that you shouldn't count people who join by letter of transfer when you're measuring church growth. Only conversions or confessions of faith should be counted as genuine growth. At both St. John's and here I've come to realize that the number of members who join by letter of transfer is the best single indicator of how outsiders, especially church shoppers, view your church. I also was taught that a minister should come into a congregation, identify the leaders, and learn how to work with those established leaders. That probably is good advice for the new minister of a small rural church, but one of the things I've learned at St. John's that also applies here is that many of a pastor's best allies, supporters, and leaders will come from among the people who joined following the arrival of that new minister. I think that is especially true if you're talking about change, church growth, or anything else that creates discontinuity with the past. It's better to win new support and enlist new leaders than to spend all your efforts trying to secure the support of inherited leaders.

"I also was taught," continued Don, "that a minister shouldn't be too aggressive in that first year of a new pastorate, but now I've learned that first year is the time to lay the foundation for what you want to happen later. Finally, I was taught in seminary to be an enabler, and that probably is a good leadership role for the pastor of a small church or for someone serving a church on a plateau, but that's not what the people in the big churches want or need. The big church needs a senior minister who is willing and able to be an initiating leader. That may have been the most difficult lesson I've had to learn."

"If you could do it all over again, what road would you choose?" asked Anne, delighted to catch Don in this reflective mood and to learn from his experience.

"Knowing what I know today, I would pick one of two alternatives," reflected Don. "If it were possible, my first choice would be to go out and start a new mission with a fifteen- to twenty-acre site at a good location with easy access, high visibility, and large enough to accommodate a congregation averaging a thousand or more at worship. That's where the future is, in those huge churches that can offer people a broad range of ministries and programs. That's another lesson I've had to unlearn. I was taught the ideal size of a congregation ranges between 140 and 165 at worship, but that's not large enough in today's world to mobilize the resources necessary to offer your generation of adults the range of choices they seek. My parents taught me the world offers you two choices, 'Take it or leave it,' and that was the basis for program planning I followed during my first dozen years in the ministry. Several years ago I finally realized the people born after the end of World War II grew up in a world that offered them a range of attractive choices. I'm not sure I could have pulled it off back then, but if I were starting over today, knowing what I think I know, I would like to be the founding pastor of a new mission that could grow into a big church and spend my entire ministry with that one congregation. I'm increasingly convinced of the value of long-term relationships."

"What would be your other choice?" questioned Anne. "You said you had two alternatives in mind."

"That's easy," answered Don. "I would spend my first ten years, more or less, on the staff of one or two very large congregations, seeking to learn and understand the distinctive characteristics of the big church, perfecting my program skills and trying to learn the role of a senior minister. Instead of learning a bunch of lessons I would have to unlearn later on, I would concentrate on becoming an expert on the nature of the large church and the distinctive role of a senior minister and then I would seek to move into a senior pastor's position."

"Are you recommending that road to me?" asked Anne.

"No, but it's one you should consider," replied Don. "What you decide will be determined by you and Jack and by the opportunities God opens up to you. I cannot define what the Lord has in mind for you. I am convinced, however, your experience here at First Church can be excellent preparation for you if and when the day comes for you to become the senior minister of a large church and I do not see any reason why you couldn't leave here and go directly to be a senior minister somewhere else."

"Don't forget I'm a woman," advised Anne. "Do you really believe it's possible for a woman, after ten or fifteen years on the staff of a congregation such as this one, to be able to go directly to a large church as the senior minister?"

"Why don't you forget about this gender factor," admonished Don, "and concentrate on ministry."

"How can I when you and everyone else keeps reminding me of the fact I'm the first woman minister in the history of this congregation?" retorted Anne.

"I understand that, at least intellectually, if not in my gut," replied Don somewhat apologetically. "Both of us need to remember a male perspective has been built into my frame of reference over the past fifty years. You look at the world from a feminist perspective, but my basic point is that you have many assets and you should see these as assets, rather than concentrating on the limitations the churches place on women in the pastoral ministry."

"Give me one example," challenged Anne.

"That's what I would like to do," replied Don. "Now that we've added staff so we can spread out the work load a little more, I would like to talk with you about a change in your responsibilities."

"What do you have in mind?" inquired Anne. "I'm happy with what I've been doing. Why change?"

"I'm happy with your work, but I have two changes in mind for now as well as for sometime later. Now that Sue is on the staff on a half-time basis to work with the new member enlistment program, you can let her work with that committee. Likewise with Harold Swanson coming on staff as a half-time minister of visitation, you should be able to cut back some on your hospital calling. Instead of three days a week, you'll only have to go to the hospitals one day a week plus every other Sunday morning. As you know I've been going to the hospital at seven o'clock every Sunday morning since I arrived, but now that we're about to go to two services, I want you to pick up on alternate Sundays and when I'm out of town. So, I have two other things in mind. One is to work with our women's fellowship. It really is in need of some help. Martha Pearson, the new president, came to me and practically begged for help. The other idea came to me yesterday afternoon as I was reflecting on the fact that you're getting married in September. You may want to talk with Jack about this before telling me yes or no, but I think we should offer a brand new adult Sunday school class two or three times a year and you could teach it. It would be a class for newlyweds. I got the idea from Bill Self at Wieuca Baptist Church in Atlanta. He and his wife have written a book for that type of class."

"You want me to work with the women's organization and you want me to teach this class for newlyweds?" questioned Anne. "Why don't you and Mary teach the class for newlyweds and ask one of the new staff members to work with the women?"

"Two reasons," replied Don. "Peter Drucker has persuaded me that whenever possible you never assign a new staff member a new major assignment. Drucker contends that newcomers to the staff should be assigned to established positions where expectations have been clearly delineated and help is available. He also advises giving new jobs to people on the staff whose behavior is known and predictable, who have earned the trust of the people and who have credibility.[1] That's why I asked you a year and a half ago to organize a special task force to build a system of new member enlistment and asked you to staff it. Now that's a going operation and Sue is on board, we can turn that over to her and ask you to take a new assignment."

"That's an interesting approach to staffing a large church," commented Anne. "I thought the usual approach is to give new assignments to new staff members."

"It is, but it's also one of those lessons I've had to unlearn since I became a senior minister," explained Don. "Drucker is right. Except for Virgil and Nellie, you're now the senior member of the staff here and so naturally I turn to a veteran to pioneer new programs and to revitalize old ones. Don't you feel like an old-timer?"

"What's your second reason?" pursued Anne, who was not quite ready to accept the fact that at age thirty with four years' tenure she was now the veteran of the program staff at First Church. "You said you had two reasons."

"I hope this doesn't offend you," continued Don carefully,

"but I think you overemphasize the limitations placed on you because you're a woman. I would like to see you place greater emphasis on the assets you bring to the ministry. One asset is the fact you're a woman. A second is you're young. Therefore, who is better qualified than a young woman to help our women's fellowship figure out why they're not reaching a generation of younger women and how to change that. A third asset, as of this October, is you're about to become a newlywed. As an experienced and exceptionally competent teacher of adult classes, who is better qualified than you to organize and teach a new class for newlyweds?"

"Yes, but it's still a male-dominated world," declared Anne who had spent thirty years learning the limitations the world places on women and four years learning a subordinate role on the staff of a large church.

Three Views of the Women's Organization

Eventually Anne agreed to accept the assignment to help the women's organization define and build a new future for itself. She soon discovered that the women held three substantially different views of the nature and role of that organization. The largest number saw it as an organization that now included six circles that met monthly and ten general meetings that typically attracted 35 to 40 women, although special programs might produce an attendance of 75 to 90. The basic organizing principles were (1) study, (2) fellowship, (3) growing old together, and (4) raising money for missions, but the amount was relatively modest in recent years.

A handful of members made it very clear they believed it should be organized around missions. "I read a statement the other day about the Women's Missionary Union in the Southern Baptist Convention," explained one of these women, "and I clipped it out because it expresses my feelings exactly. Let me read it to you. 'We are not a woman's organization that happens to support missions. We are a missions organization that happens to be composed of women. Missions is our purpose, our lifeblood, our heritage, and our future.' I like that and I think that should be our slogan," she concluded as she folded the newspaper clipping and returned it to her purse.

A third group of members, when questioned by Anne, were not clear on the central purpose. Some saw it as the women's equivalent of the Men's Club. Others saw it simply as one more program group at First Church which happened to be composed of women. A few urged that it become an aggressive advocate of feminist causes. Several simply shrugged and replied, "Well, doesn't every church have a women's organization?" As she listened to this group, their comments reminded Anne of when she was a child and looked into a kaleidoscope. As she rotated it, the pattern changed. As she listened to this third group, she heard the definitions of role and purpose change with each speaker.

Anne had discovered two facts about the group life of churches as she had struggled to help build a system for new member enlistment at First Church. The first was that the groups that often experience the greatest difficulty in enlisting new members tend to (a) be composed of people who have known one another for a long time, (b) display a strong past-orientation, (c) be highly relational, (d) be organized around study and/or fellowship as central values, (e) display a person-centered rather than task-oriented orientation, (f) be ones in which the organizational structure appears to be more important than the task, and (g) if issue-centered, be concerned with a variety of issues.

By contrast, Anne also had learned that the groups most likely to enlist new members are those (a) that are advancing a cause, (b) that feel a strong need to enlist additional members in order to fulfill their purpose or accomplish their task, (c) in which the organizational structure is a means-to-an-end and secondary to the task, (d) that challenge people with specific, meaningful, attainable, and measurable goals, (e) that have the benefit of strong and continuing leadership, (f) that focus on a single issue, and (g) that enlist people to help pioneer a new venture.

After several months of study the special task force Anne had asked to be appointed recommended:

1. The central focus be shifted from the women's organization as a whole to the several circles.

2. The goal would be to organize three new circles a year for the next three years.

3. The members of the existing circles be asked to continue those long-established circles, but 20 percent of the members of each circle (that translated into three to six members from each circle) be challenged to leave that circle and help pioneer new circles.

4. The new circles would include three organized around missions, two to be organized as Mothers' Clubs for new mothers, two would be organized around crafts, one would be a quilting circle (this became the largest and the only truly multi-generational circle), and one would be left to be organized around unforeseen needs.

5. An annual bazaar would be held with all the proceeds to be allocated to missions. The two crafts circles would take turns planning and organizing this, but every circle would be encouraged to participate.

6. General meetings, each with a distinctive and clearly defined theme, would be held quarterly and all these would be evening events.

7. The executive committee would consist of a president, vice president, and program director elected at large at the spring general meeting, plus one representative selected by each circle.

8. After three years a special review committee would be appointed by the president to evaluate what had happened and would recommend the next steps.

This proposal aroused opposition from those (a) who remembered that nine years earlier the governing board at First Church had outlawed all fund-raising events such as bazaars, (b) who believed new people should be directed into existing circles, (c) who opposed the decentralized structure, (d) who were convinced the central focus should be missions and only missions, and (e) who were convinced too many changes were being made too rapidly at First Church already and the women's organization should be a haven of stability immune to change.

After three months of intense discussion this action plan was adopted, partly on its merits and partly because of the absence of any attractive alternative.

Anne supported it because she believed strongly in the old adage of "new groups for new people"; she saw the bazaar as an attractive entry for new members who wanted to express their creativity through their hands; she was convinced that giving people choices was necessary in a congregation as diverse and heterogeneous as this one; she saw this as a means of sharply expanding the emphasis on missions (five years later each of the three new circles organized around missions had taken one work camp trip to a mission field outside North America and the oldest of these three circles was planning its second trip); and she believed the bazaar would be a means of demonstrating this was a semiautonomous organization that was self-governing, self-supporting, and self-propagating rather than tied to the past or controlled by the actions of the governing board of nine years earlier.

Six years following the somewhat reluctant approval of this action plan (a) those six long-established circles were now three, (b) fourteen new circles had been organized of which twelve survived those critical first two years, (c) twelve of the eighteen women on the executive committee were under thirty-seven years of age, (d) the governing board had yet to officially discuss the legitimacy of the annual bazaar, (e) the amount of money contributed to missions annually had risen from $1,650 to $18,000 in six years, (f) forty-three different women at First Church, including twenty-two who were past sixty-five years of age, had gone on one or more work camp mission trips outside North America, (g) more than two dozen women from other churches in the denomination had come to study what First Church had done to revitalize its women's organization, (h) after four years Anne had been able to gradually reduce the time she allocated to the women's organization to an average of seven to nine hours a month, including the time she devoted to helping pioneer one new circle every year, and (i) the two largest, best attended and most festive special events were the two surprise baby showers the executive committee organized for Anne, one in the second year of this new action plan and one in the fifth.

During the first shower, which was attended by nearly four hundred people one Tuesday evening, Don whispered to

Anne, "I told you to build on your assets. They would never do this for a male pastor."

The revitalized women's organization also became Anne's number-one support group. The Board at First Church adopted as an official policy that any pregnant member of the staff was entitled to one month of maternity leave with full pay for each year of service on the staff with a maximum of three months. Subsequently one influential and highly articulate, long-time member criticized this as an extravagant policy that discriminated against men. When this became known, more than two hundred women vowed they would completely ignore him or even acknowledge his presence in a group until after Anne's baby was born. When he finally realized he was being subjected to this silent treatment, he complained to his wife. She retorted, "Consider yourself lucky. The original proposal was to take you out and hang you from that oak tree on the south side of the church." It still is possible in this changing world to build a cohesive and unified women's organization if there is an attractive rallying point. It also helps to have a clearly identified enemy.

The Sunday Church School

One of Anne's allies in the revitalization of the women's organization was Susan Riedel, a new part-time staff member who had picked up Anne's responsibilities in new member enlistment. Susan helped many new members find a home in one of those new circles where they could meet and make new friends.

Another ally was Barbara Cook who, during Don's second year, had come on the staff to develop and oversee a package of ministries with families that included teenagers. Barbara, who was 57 when she joined the staff, had been divorced when she was 28 and the mother of two young children. At 36 she had married a widower who had two teenagers. He had died a week after Barbara's fifty-second birthday. Barbara had firsthand knowledge about stepchildren, blended families, stepparenting, and being a single parent. In addition, she had gone to graduate school after her second husband's death and had earned a master's degree in family systems theory to go with her degree in education and twelve years' experience teaching in high school.

Pastor Johnson and the personnel committee had concluded she had the ideal qualifications for this new position. Don's only reservation was that this meant running counter to Peter Drucker's advice against asking a new staff person to accept a new assignment.

When Neva's resignation was accepted, this posed the question, Who will staff the Sunday church school? This really was the issue, since the Christian education program at First Church consisted of little except that dwindling Sunday school of twelve classes when Don arrived. Neva really was a paid Sunday school superintendent, not the director of a larger program.

Don's response, which few were able to comprehend, much less support, was the suggestion that instead of conceptualizing the Sunday church school as an end in itself, it be seen as one component of a series of mutually reinforcing ministries. These would include new member enlistment, the yet-to-be-developed threefold package of ministries with families that included (a) preschool children, (b) elementary school age children, and (c) youth, the women's organization, the assimilation of new adult members, the adult Bible study classes, and the ministry of music.

Within four years after Barbara's arrival, the Sunday church school at First Church had grown from twelve to three dozen classes. This list included ten classes in the children's division, two different classes for junior high youth, three different classes for high school youth, two classes for newlyweds (each of which originally was intended to be integrated into existing adult classes after a year, but several classes decided to continue as couples classes), the Phoenix class for adults in their second or subsequent marriage, the issue-centered Forum Class, two faith journey classes (both of which had started as classes for newlyweds), a class for new stepparents, a class for single parents, a class for young childless adults both never married and married, a class founded in 1950 of young couples that now was composed largely of retired couples, widows, and a couple of widowers, a traditional adult Bible study class that traced its origin back to 1960, another adult class that was basically a book review group that was first organized in 1967, a class composed of parents of preschool children, a class of parents who for the first time in their lives were living with a teenager, a large class composed mostly of choir members taught by the new minister of music, two classes that had begun as new member orientation classes a couple of years earlier and decided they wanted to continue as adult classes, an intergenerational class with members ranging in age from 15 to 88 that focused on what the Scriptures had to say about current social issues, and a large Pastor's Class taught by Don that had grown to an average attendance of over one hundred by the fourth year.

The Pastor's Class

This class was designed on a model Pastor Johnson had developed back at St. John's Church. It met during the Sunday school hour and was designed to be an easy entry class for newcomers, introverted people, those who wanted to become better acquainted with the senior minister, people who were comfortable with a lecture-type class, those who could not attend every Sunday, people who had yet to decide whether they wanted to join a "permanent" class, and many others. Each week's lesson was designed to stand alone. It was not necessary to have been present last week to comprehend today's lesson. There were no references to next week such as, "Let's hold that and we'll talk about that next Sunday." A person could come and know there would be no risk of embarrassment. Questions and comments were encouraged, but no one was ever asked, "Tell us what you think about that." The design enabled those who so desired to attend for five years without ever speaking.

The hour was preceded by refreshments and ten or fifteen minutes of fellowship, but no one was required to come early. The class met in a very large room right off the main entrance and was easy to find. This room was filled with a variety of comfortable chairs that offered people a wide range of choices in an informal seating arrangement. Don used a wireless microphone and the room had an excellent public address system so the teacher could move around freely. Don made a point of beginning promptly at nine-thirty, the scheduled beginning time, and stopped fifty minutes later.

At both churches Don made sure the class included three or four articulate members who felt comfortable coloring outside the lines. They were encouraged to ask combative questions, to disagree, and to challenge. That gave others permission as well as kept this from becoming a fifty-minute monologue. The First Church maverick personalities included an attorney, a veterinarian, a used car salesman, and an elementary school teacher, all of whom (a) were good friends with the senior minister and with one another, (b) loved to argue, (c) could accept being the butt of a joke, (d) never completely agreed with one another, (e) possessed a great sense of humor, (f) enjoyed putting the senior minister on the spot when they caught an inconsistency, and (g) arrived early to enjoy their coffee and greet newcomers.

Either the attorney or the veterinarian substituted for Don when he had to be absent and both were highly competent teachers. The lesson, regardless of who taught the class, always was about a passage or a concept from the Bible. It was a Bible study class. Thanks to the contributions and the presence of these four mavericks, the class would be interrupted by a roar of laughter at least a half dozen times every Sunday morning. The only dull Sundays during these first six years came on two occasions when all four were absent on the same Sunday.

This class met every Sunday morning, including the summer, and it was a tremendous asset in the assimilation of newcomers. It also was a great place for persons who lived alone to come and find a feeling of family. Don usually closed the class with prayer at twenty minutes past ten and left the room about fifteen minutes later, but except for those who were in the choir or were pulled away by children, most of the members stayed to talk and finish off the refreshments for a half hour after the end of the lesson. By the end of Don's tenth year attendance had climbed to close to two hundred, the capacity of that room, and had to be moved to the fellowship hall.

This class was Don's favorite illustration of large group

dynamics.[2] It also demonstrated the need in the large church to offer people a choice among several entry points and the value of conceptualizing this large church as a congregation of congregations. When this class moved into the fellowship hall in Don's tenth year, it had grown to the point that, in terms of Sunday morning attendance, it was larger than four out of five Protestant congregations on the North American continent.

Guiding Principles

In rebuilding the Sunday school, Don, Barbara, Anne, and the other staff members at First Church were guided by several principles which they all supported.

1. A basic assumption should be projected that *everyone* was expected to be present for two hours on Sunday morning. This is in contrast to those large churches that project (a) the assumption that Sunday school is for children and worship for adults or (b) schedule worship and Sunday school for the same hour, or (c) offer few adult classes. This first assumption led them to concentrate first on expanding the choices for adults. That forced the subsequent expansion of the children's program. Children adopt the behavior patterns they see modeled by adults.

2. They concluded it would be wise to offer a range of different types of adult classes rather than simply divide adults by age, gender, and marital status.[3]

3. They emphasized the concept of religious journeys and stages of faith development in their planning and designed classes for people at different stages of the faith or at different points in their pilgrimage.[4]

4. They placed a heavy emphasis on responding to the hunger of adults for Bible study, but offered choices in what was taught and how it was taught.[5] An example was one of the three classes offered teenagers. It was a Bible study class and drew members from all four grades of high school, but fewer than one-third of the high school youth enrolled in that class. A second example is the class taught by Don Johnson. When the attendance passed two hundred in Don's tenth year and the move was made to the fellowship hall, that meant that

seven-eighths of the 1,600 members were not interested in being a part of this class. In designing the new system the staff accepted as a fact of life that the majority of youth and the vast majority of adults would stay away from any one class. The staff accepted diversity and built on that, rather than attempting to pretend it did not exist or to combat it.

5. They designed classes to be points of entry into First Church, to be places to meet and make new friends, to serve as mutual support and caring groups, and to be places to serve as well as to be educational experiences.

6. They placed a great emphasis on the value of long-term relationships and all except five of the adult classes were designed to be permanent and continuing groups.

7. To offset the natural tendency for these permanent classes to become exclusionary groups, they encouraged every adult class to plan at least six or eight social gatherings annually with the expectation these social events could be entry points for new members into that adult class.

8. On the assumption that would not always work their backup system included (a) Don's easy entry class, (b) the creation of at least two new adult classes every year to enable new people to help pioneer a new class, and (c) every class appointing a person to be responsible, on a one-to-one basis, for the assimilation of new people into that class.

9. They encouraged every adult class to begin with refreshments and fellowship fifteen minutes before the beginning of the Sunday school hour. One result was that in several classes that became a half-hour period and the Sunday school hour shrunk to forty or forty-five minutes.

10. The staff also attempted to offer several adult classes to meet people where they were in their life cycle.

One of the price tags of this successful effort to expand the Sunday school was a mounting wave of criticism, especially from the newer members, on the lack of foresight in the remodeling of the fellowship hall. It was now obvious to everyone that project should have provided for at least six or eight additional classrooms. It really is hard to please everyone!

Chapter Six

Five of Pastor Johnson's primary concerns when he came to First Church were directed at what happened on Sunday morning. These were improving the ratio of worship-attendance-to-membership, developing a larger and more extensive ministry of music, rebuilding the Sunday school, increasing the amount of off-street parking, and providing a more inviting place for people to gather and socialize before and after worship. The successful Miracle Sunday financial campaign enabled First Church to go ahead with plans that took care of the last two of these five items.

Just before the end of Don's first year the forty-three-year-old Paul Kramer joined the staff as a full-time minister of music. Paul's first step was to transform the chancel choir into a religious community that soon grew to nearly sixty members.

When Don interviewed Paul, one of the first questions he asked was, "If you join our staff, what will be the first change you will attempt to introduce here?" Without hesitating Paul replied, "I will organize and teach a new adult Sunday school class that will meet in the choir room at the beginning of the Sunday school hour and invite all the members of the present choir to join that class as well as other people. I will attempt to build that class into a closely knit, supportive, loving, caring Christian community. Out of that class I would hope to get at least forty people who will constitute the adult choir plus at least a dozen others who will help with the rest of the music program. If you'll pardon my lack of humility, I am a good teacher as well as a good musician. I've followed that method in both of the churches I've served and I think it will work here."

Don had never heard of that idea before, but it intrigued him so much that he forgot all the reservations he had always carried about full-time ministers of music. When John Owen resigned, Don had been thinking in terms of building a music staff consisting of five or six part-time people plus the part-time organist who had been with First Church for nearly twenty years.

Later in that same interview Don asked, "We're thinking about going to two worship services here. How do you see that affecting your work?"

"As long as the first one is over at least five minutes before the beginning of the Sunday school hour, I don't see a problem. If, however, you're thinking about the new service being at the Sunday school hour, I might as well leave now. That's too much competition for people's time for me. When you put worship, the Sunday school, and the ministry of music into direct competition with one another, you can count me out," explained Paul. "I can live very comfortably with a schedule of worship followed by Sunday school followed by a second service, but not if you want to jam all three into two hours."

Three years later when Don proposed going to three worship services on Sunday morning, the new minister of music reminded him of that conversation. During the first three years of his tenure, however, Paul turned out to be the answer to a senior minister's prayer. The only continuing point of friction, which surfaced no more than two or three times a week, came as Paul insisted all hymns for Sunday morning worship should be "good" hymns, while Don was adamant in his opinion that every service include at least one hymn that nearly everyone knew, loved, and enjoyed singing.

One of Paul's first moves after coming on staff was to court and win the support of the four volunteers who had been carrying the responsibility for the two children's choirs. All four had been accustomed to being ignored, criticized, and neglected, and they were flattered to receive so much attention. Within six months one had agreed to help organize a new drama group of older teenagers. A second had volunteered to help organize and direct a cadre of volunteers who would find the money necessary to purchase new robes for the chancel choir, and a third had agreed to organize and oversee a choir mothers' group that would be the support group for the ministry of music with children. The fourth, who was an excellent children's choir director, was asked to continue in that role with the promise that beginning with the next budget, she would be paid a modest stipend.

When the committee that had selected Paul Kramer had asked him about salary, he replied, "If you want me to do everything, I'll need a cash salary of $68,000 plus the normal other benefits." As the members of the committee picked themselves up off the floor after hearing that request, Paul continued, "But if you want me to build a good music program, I'll come for $30,000 a year, but you'll have to include at least $10,000 a year in the budget for other staff, not counting what you pay the organist."

One member of the committee, who had been prepared for the change from the $6,000 a year First Church had been paying John Owen, to perhaps $24,000 for a full-time choir director, was so overcome by Paul's brashness that he almost choked while trying to express his objections. One of the choir members on the committee interrupted his objections by explaining, "During the past twenty-five years First Church has saved nearly a quarter of a million dollars by trying to get by with a very limited music program. Maybe the time has come to spend some of the money we've saved for a good program."

Four years after Paul's arrival, the music program, which was described by various members as "superb," "inspiring," "extravagant," "the best thing that's happened here since the fire," "the tail that wags the dog," "beyond comprehension," "Paul Kramer's little empire," and "a budget buster" included (a) a religious community that had grown to nearly eighty people and completely filled the choir rehearsal room during Sunday school, (b) a choir of thirty-five to forty voices that sang on forty-five Sundays a year at the second service, (c) a choir of twenty-five to thirty voices, a few of whom also were members of the other choir that sang at the eight-thirty service, (d) a high school vocal choir, (e) a high school handbell choir, (f) four other handbell choirs, each with its own director, one of which was restricted to people age sixty-five and over who spent twenty Sundays a year serving as the visiting choir for very small churches, within a seventy-five-mile radius, that did not have their own choir, (g) a music encounter program using Orff instruments (purchased with memorial funds) for three- and four-year-olds who met mornings on Tuesdays and Fridays, (h) a parallel music encounter group for five- and six-year-olds who met after school two days a week, (i) a junior high choir, (j) an older teenage drama group, (k) a brass ensemble which, seven years later, had grown into a twenty-four-person orchestra, (l) an adult drama group, (m) three children's choirs, (n) a ten-person flute choir, (o) nine part-time paid music staff members with combined salaries of $29,800, and (p) a half-time secretary to the minister of music.

During Dr. Bennington's last year the total expenditures for music, including John Owen's salary, had been equal to almost exactly 2 percent of that $405,000 budget.

The budget for Don's sixth year at First Church had more than doubled to $938,500 and 10 percent of that was allocated to the ministry of music. Whenever this dramatic increase was discussed, some members pointed out that was excessive, extravagant, and unnecesary. Others attempted to explain that the greatly expanded music program was a big reason behind the increase in worship attendance and the increase in worship attendance was the basic reason for that increase in member giving. Don Johnson was happy with the results and agreed the benefits justified the cost.

The Schedule

One of Don's first initiatives was to schedule a survey of worship attendance for the last three Sundays in October and the first Sunday in November following his arrival. He had designed a 3″ x 5″ card for this purpose when he was at St. John's Church and used that same format. For four consecutive Sundays a couple of minutes of each worship service were allocated to asking everyone present to fill out a 3″ x 5″ card.

White cards were used the first Sunday, green the second, yellow the third, and pink the fourth. This made it easier when the time came to tabulate the results. Everyone present, including all the children, was asked to write on this card their name, to check one of five categories of their relationships to First Church (confirmed member, child, first-time visitor, repeat visitor, or constituent) gender, distance from their place of residence to First Church (less than one mile, one to two miles, two to three miles, three to five miles, beyond five miles), and, if a member, whether they had joined in 1977 or earlier or 1978 or later. (Soon after his arrival Don had determined that one-half of the current membership had joined in 1977 or earlier and one-half had joined in 1978 or later. Thus members were being asked to indicate whether they belonged to the newest one-half of the membership or were among the long-tenured half of the membership.)

With the help of seven volunteers, three of whom enjoyed the chance to utilize their computer skills, this table was produced.

CHURCH ATTENDANCE SURVEY

	Joined 1977 or earlier	Joined 1978 or later	Total
Members attending one Sunday	77	63	140
Members attending two Sundays	71	54	125
Members attending three Sundays	69	38	107
Members attending four Sundays	52	79	131
Members attending at least once	269	234	503
Average number of first-time visitors			19
Average number of repeat visitors			27
Average number of constituents			17
Average number of children (0-13 years old)			16
Usher count of attendance (average) = 388			

The results of this survey confirmed many of Don's hunches as well as several of his fears. While attendance had begun to climb slowly following his arrival that summer, this survey suggested that most of the growth had come from (a) an increase in the number of visitors, (b) the frequent attendance of the three dozen new members who had joined since Don's arrival, and (c) an increase in the number of children present for worship from an average of four or five to sixteen.

The bad news began with the fact that over three hundred members did not attend even once during this four-Sunday period. This confirmed Don's hunch that the membership roll included many inactive members. The second bit of bad news was that more longer-tenure members than newer members attended at least once. This confirmed Don's hunch that the process for the assimilation of new members had been less than fully effective for the past several years. The third bit of bad news was that among the members who did attend at least once, those attending once or twice outnumbered those who attended three or four Sundays in that four-Sunday period.

This survey confirmed Don's hunch that this was a predominantly female congregation. The American population, age twenty and older, is 53 percent female and 47 percent male. The average attendance of the members at First Church was 59 percent female and 41 percent male.

This survey also confirmed Don's hunch about the geographical dispersal of the active membership. While fewer than one-half of the members attending two or more Sundays who had joined in 1977 or earlier lived beyond two miles from the building, nearly three-quarters of those attending at least twice who joined in 1978 or later lived at least three miles from the building.

Perhaps most important of all, this survey provided Don with the factual data he needed to initiate several changes. The most difficult was his proposal to eliminate Children's Church. This had been one of Dr. Bennington's favorite innovations. The children, age twelve and younger, were urged to leave the worship service after about fifteen minutes and go to another room for the remainder of the hour. Don believed strongly that the most powerful pedagogical force is modeling. He was convinced children are greatly influenced by what they see adults doing, so he believed they should be in worship the entire hour. He also was convinced that could be a meaningful experience for children. In addition, he wanted to project the image that everyone was expected to be present for *both* the Sunday school hour *and* for worship. He was convinced that Children's Church encouraged parents of young children to come for only one hour.

A second change this new senior minister introduced was to expand the schedule to begin with worship followed by Sunday church school followed by a second worship experience.

This was greeted by the response, "That will split our church in two congregations." Don's response was, "This church already is divided into three congregations, approximately 250 members who attend regularly, another 250 who attend less frequently, and over 300 who rarely attend." The attendance survey provided the data for that statement.

The third change he proposed was to create an attractive schedule that would give people choices. Don saw that was one way to increase both the number of people who attended and the frequency of their attendance.[1] In addition to offering people a choice of an early or late worship experience, Don wanted to schedule adult classes at all three hours. This would allow those volunteers who wanted to teach in the Sunday church school, to be in worship, and to participate in an adult class to be able to do so. The proposed schedule also would enable people to have a choice of choirs since the chancel choir always sang at the second service and other choirs provided the music at the first hour. It also would offer people a choice of worship followed by Sunday school or Sunday school followed by worship.

It worked. That created a new question. Should we go to three worship services on Sunday morning? This provoked immediate opposition from (a) the leaders and staff of the Sunday school who were convinced this would undercut their program and (b) Paul Kramer, the minister of music who categorically refused to leave his adult class to attend, much less direct a choir at the Sunday school hour.

After many months of discussion, and three years after the change to a two-service schedule, a new proposal emerged. The heart of this proposal was to offer people choices. The theme was, "You are invited to come for four hours, but if you want to come only for three hours, this schedule also encourages that response."

The new schedule began with breakfast at seven o'clock on Sunday morning. On the typical Sunday morning a handful of people straggled in a few minutes after seven. About fifteen minutes later two dozen adults came, quickly went through the serving line, and by seven-thirty were in their room for a two-hour Bible study class. A little later several members of the adult choir that sang at the first service appeared. They were followed by those who came early, either for breakfast before their eight-thirty class or those who wanted breakfast before the first worship service. The serving line remained open until nine to accommodate those who wanted breakfast before the regular Sunday school hour, choir members for the second service, and those who wanted breakfast before going to the second worship service.

Later on, as he explained the value of breakfast to other pastors, Don pointed out three major fringe benefits. First, this was a great time to strengthen the relationships among newcomers and old-timers and among those who came at an early hour and those who appeared a little later. Second, the eighty minutes before he left to robe for that first service gave Don the opportunity for carrying out a lot of pastoral care with no time spent on travel.

Third, and in some respect the most important fringe benefit, was that this gave a highly visible, rewarding, and unifying role for the Men's Fellowship at First Church. It usually is easier to build a women's group around study than it is to use that as the central organizing principle for an all-male group. Most men's groups benefit from a "project" that enables them to express their creativity with their hands.

The Men's Fellowship was persuaded to accept this assignment and as a result (a) their organization grew from fifteen to twenty men to over fifty as each team of men, every eighth Sunday, took the responsibility for preparing and serving breakfast and cleaning up afterward, (b) newcomers felt needed and welcomed as they helped implement what had become a group goal of the Men's Fellowship, (c) newcomers and long-time members became friends by working together on a common task, (d) a four-hour commitment on Sunday morning (actually many were present for six hours eight or nine times a year) was made, (e) the work load was spread out among many, (f) an average of nearly $8,000 was raised every year for world missions from the difference between their costs and the price of the meal, (g) people felt good about the huge investment in the new kitchen that was a part of the fellowship hall renovation several years earlier, and (h) it offered an incentive that brought many people, especially those who lived alone, to First Church for fellowship, a sense of inclusion, and a chance to be loved.

The opportunity to have breakfast at church and the expansion of the music program that always provided a minimum of two music groups at the eight-thirty worship experience were two big reasons that kept the attendance at the first service from dropping when the schedule was expanded to include three worship experiences every Sunday morning.

One of the predictable patterns that occurred in the early weeks was that the first Sunday breakfast consisted of a choice of rolls, doughnuts, juice, and coffee. The second team expanded that to include cold cereal. The third team expanded the menu to include toast. The fourth team added scrambled eggs. The fifth team added pancakes. The sixth team added hot cereal. The seventh team felt intimidated. The eighth team declared, "That's enough!" When their turn came around the second time, the first team added fresh fruit, just to make sure no one perceived them as inferior or inadequate.

The competitive nature of the new game was criticized by many and enhanced by several wives who came when it was their husband's turn, but everyone had fun, ate well, and worship attendance continued to climb. Many years later when the Johnsons left First Church, the second biggest of the several farewell events scheduled to wish Mary and Don a fond farewell was the breakfast party on their last Sunday.

This new four-period schedule began with breakfast and included three worship experiences, but it also both encouraged and required an expansion of the music program and an increase in the choices available to teenagers and adults for educational experiences. One result was that several teenagers came to the first worship service, worked in the children's division of the Sunday school hour, and participated in an intergenerational Bible study group at the last hour.

Another result of this emphasis on being present for either three or four hours, plus the range of choices offered at every hour, reduced the visibility of the "one-hour package" that was available at the Sunday school hour when children could be in Sunday school while their parents were in worship.

On a long-term basis one of the most significant results was that while children were welcome at all three services, the eight-thirty hour became the one attended by fifty to seventy children on a typical Sunday. The appeal of this service was enhanced by the possibility of going to church for breakfast, the presence of one of the children's choirs on forty or more Sundays a year, the fact that the family could be on its way to Grandma's or the lake by ten-thirty, the new custom that the people who received the offering at the first service were not the ushers, but one or two families with young children helping to pass the offering plates, the children's sermon (also offered at eleven o'clock, but not at the second service), and always one hymn that could be sung and understood by children. Some parents added it was easier for their children to sit still early in the morning than if they came to worship after Sunday school.

Another result that was more apparent to the staff than to most members was that the second service gradually became the major entry point for new young adults who either were not married or were childless. Some of them stayed for an adult class at eleven o'clock, but a larger number came for breakfast at eight-thirty to nine and did not participate in an adult class. This pattern was reinforced by Paul Kramer's willingness to find someone else to organize and create a young adult choir that sang at that second service. While the first and third services usually included two to five musical groups on the typical Sunday morning, that young adult choir often was the only musical group at the second service.

Expanding the Range of Choices

One of the most difficult lessons Don Johnson had learned during his three decades as a pastor was that no matter what the new idea is, it probably will not work. His response to this depressing discovery was to build as much redundancy as possible into every system. Thus, when he proposed the new four-period schedule, he sought to build into it as many reasons as possible to make it work.

The day after the staff meeting at which Don had introduced the possibility of expanding the Sunday morning schedule to include breakfast plus three worship exeriences, Anne dropped into Don's office and asked, "Oh, wise and farsighted leader, what's going to happen to the class you've been teaching during the Sunday school hour if we go to this new schedule?"

"I'm delighted you used the first person plural in the last part of your question," instantly replied Don. "That's what will make it work! When *we* go to the new schedule, *we* can make it work because as you explained to me many years ago when I first arrived, you would like to preach every Sunday and with this schedule *we* can give you that opportunity. I just assumed you would understand that the middle hour would be the service at which you would preach."

"Every Sunday?" questioned Anne.

"No, not every Sunday," explained Don. "Whenever a month has five Sundays, I'll take the middle hour and you will preach at the first and third services and you can teach my Pastor's Class on those four Sundays every year."

"But if I preach at the middle hour on forty-eight Sundays a year," responded Anne with suppressed glee as she sought to point out the two flaws in the plan, "that soon will mean there'll be only a handful of people coming at the first and third hours. You also have to realize that if I preach at the middle hour, that may wipe out all the adult Sunday School classes now meeting at that hour."

"Motherhood certainly has enhanced your humility,"

retorted Don, "but the music program should continue to attract at least a couple of dozen to the first and third hours and besides that, our nave won't accommodate that many people."

"As you can see, I'm absolutely delighted with the chance to preach every Sunday," exclaimed Anne, "but why didn't you bring this up yesterday at staff meeting?"

"First of all, you won't be preaching every Sunday," explained Don. "We expect you'll have one Sunday vacation every year. Second, I didn't mention it yesterday because today's your birthday, and I thought this would be a good birthday present."

The seven most common reactions to the proposal that the new schedule would mean both Don and Anne would be preaching on most Sundays of the year were (a) "Great!" (b) "Why should we pay for the time for two sermon preparations every week when one minister could preach the same sermon at all three services?" (c) "Why not schedule Anne to preach at the hour I usually come and let Don preach at the other two services?" (d) "This is a guaranteed method of undercutting what appears to be a remarkably harmonious relationship between two very effective pastors and turning that into a highly competitive relationship," (e) "Does this mean we're 'showcasing' Anne so she can get her own church?" (f) "I've never heard of such a dumb idea as this is!" and (g) "Why not?"

As a matter of fact, Don was introducing to First Church a concept that had become increasingly common among large congregations in the 1980s. The key ingredient is that the staff must include two ministers who are highly competent in the pulpit.

The basic assumption is that it is impossible for one person to prepare and preach a sermon that will be a meaningful component of the worship experience for everyone. This had come home clearly to Don several years earlier while he and Mary were on vacation. As they drove away from the church where they had worshiped that morning, Mary had exclaimed, "That was a marvelous sermon!" Don's immediate response was, "I didn't think it was very good at all. He rarely referred to his text, and he rambled all over the landscape.

Twice I thought he had come to an excellent concluding point, but he kept on talking." "You're talking about the outline and the mechanics," exclaimed Mary, "and all I'm saying is he spoke to what was in my heart this morning."

At first Don had concluded that he was guilty of professional jealousy, but time helped him understand that was not the issue. He had noticed, for example, that whenever Anne preached, a couple of dozen members were always present, but these same members came less than one-half the time when Don preached. Likewise he and Anne had commented to each other that several of the most faithful attenders often were absent when Anne preached. Earlier he had discovered that several of the people who reportedly rarely missed worship during Dr. Bennington's tenure became far less frequent attenders following Don's arrival. Likewise some members who were out on the fringe during his predecessor's era became regular attenders after Don came to First Church.

Thus, when the time came to design the new schedule, Don found himself with a garden full of reasons to ask Anne to preach at the middle service. This allowed him to continue with his adult class. It gave people another set of choices. It increased the chances of Anne's staying at First Church in addition to fulfilling her number-one wish. It was a means of acknowledging the diversity within the membership. It gave a distinctive identity to that new middle service, which soon was widely identified as "Anne's service."

To those who challenged, "Why should we have to pay for two sermon preparations every week?" Don also had a range of responses. To some he said, "The vast majority of Protestant churches on this continent average fewer than a hundred at worship. If they can afford to pay for the preparation of a new sermon every week, a congregation like ours that averages well over five hundred at worship certainly should be able to afford two sermon preparations a week." To others he explained simply, "Here at First Church we believe in giving people a choice." To a few he pointed out, "This seems to be one of the best ways to guarantee that the new service at the middle hour will attract enough people to make it viable." At other times Don simply asked, "Please give it a year and let's see what happens."

Subsequently, the debate arose around which was the number-one reason for the doubling of worship attendance. Some argued it was the expanded schedule. Others claimed Anne's preaching was the biggest factor. Many pointed to Don's competence and creativity. A large number declared the expanded music program was the number-one reason. Several pointed back to the renovation of the fellowship hall and the expansion of the parking area as the key. A few argued that the building of a large and competent program staff was the most critical single factor. A great many were convinced the expanded educational ministry was the most crucial single change. A couple of dozen men clearly understood the influence of offering breakfast as the biggest factor behind the increase in attendance. Don agreed with all of them. He disagreed only with those who insisted on a single factor analysis of any complex issue.

Sunday Morning Fellowship

From a ministerial perspective Pastor Don Johnson had long been convinced that every Christian should gather as part of a worshiping community every Sunday morning to praise God, to offer thanks to the Creator, to hear the gospel, to celebrate the resurrection of Jesus Christ, to learn more about Christ as Lord and Savior, and to be receptive to the power of the Holy Spirit. That should be sufficient motivation. His experiences as a pastor, however, had convinced Don that was not always sufficient motivation to bring everyone to worship. Therefore, he was reasonably comfortable with the concept of redundancy. That was one reason he wanted a strong music program and a big adult Sunday school. Redundancy and expanding the range of reasons for coming to church was part of his strategy for introducing that new worship experience with Anne as the preacher at the middle hour. Breakfast also provided a redundant pull to bring people who otherwise would have almost made it to church that morning. Don also worked hard in sermon preparation. People had a right to want to be fed spiritually.

Pastor Johnson also recognized the importance of fellowship in building a worshiping community, in introducing new people into that community, and in enhancing the caring nature of that called-out community.

Among the questions raised about the Sunday morning fellowship period three recur repeatedly. Most common is when it should be. "Should we schedule this period before or after worship?" For those congregations with a large adult Sunday school or with two worship experiences on Sunday morning, the most frequent answer is immediately before the last worship service of the morning. That, however, usually produces two objections. "One of the primary reasons for the fellowship period is to provide a warm and friendly greeting to first-time visitors. Most of them don't arrive until a few minutes before worship so that won't work!" The second is, "Most of our adult members don't come to Sunday school, and many of them won't come early simply for a cup of coffee."

One response to these and similar objections is to amend the schedule to allow time for a fellowship period both before and after worship. At First Church the principle of redundancy had caused Don and the other leaders to offer an attractive opportunity for fellowship before and after each service. For nearly two hundred people that was breakfast, for a few it was the period following the first worship experience, for many it was the period between Sunday school and the last worship service, while for others who came only to that last worship service the fellowship period followed worship. Don recognized that no matter what is planned, it will not work perfectly for all, so he designed a schedule with four periods for fellowship—and that, of course, missed those who failed to appear on Sunday morning.

A second common issue is the lack of an attractive room on the same level with the sanctuary that is easy to find. The ideal arrangement, as one congregation in Wisconsin has demonstrated, is to design the building so everyone leaving the nave walks through the fellowship area on the way to claim their coats or to reach a convenient exit. In that congregation nearly every attender stays for twenty to fifty minutes after worship.

The renovation and expansion of the fellowship hall at First Church provided that attractive and convenient gathering room. For those without that valuable asset, it may be useful to reflect on alternative means of increasing participation.

The first step is to post a redundant set of signs that direct people to the appropriate place and also state the time. The signs should be designed to be easily understood by a first-time visitor, and it may be useful to provide a space for insertion of a card highlighting this week's special attraction. The second most useful step is to provide name tags for everyone. The third step, if space permits, is to offer the convenience of the appropriate number of lightweight, easy-to-move, comfortable individual chairs that *do not fold* (stacking chairs are acceptable). Next, always offer people a choice of at least four beverages. Fifth, secure one gregarious volunteer host and one extroverted volunteer hostess every week who will encourage everyone to wear a name tag, welcome strangers, and introduce those who do not appear to be well acquainted to the most sociable members.

After those five basic steps have been implemented, the next stage in reinforcing an attractive fellowship experience might include several possibilities from this list: (1) encourage groups and organizations, such as adult classes, the choir, the women's organization, or the youth fellowship to set up tables or booths to enlist volunteers or sell tickets or secure reservations or sell merchandise, (2) post on one wall a changing variety of conversation starters such as posters, maps, charts, 11″ x 14″ and larger photographs, clippings, and announcements, (3) schedule one or two action events every week such as a six- or seven-minute musical performance by a violinist or a vocal group or a brass quartet or a puppet show or a juggler or a mime or a color slide exhibit or a clown ministry by teenagers or a conversationalist who will discuss a publicized-in-advance topic, (4) if you expect more than fifty at any one time, provide food as well as a choice of beverage and use two widely separated tables for refreshments (people who are eating both attract other people and create clusters that block traffic), (5) legitimatize the concept that many adults simply like to sit and watch people, (6) if space permits, create a couple of attractive 90 degree corners of furniture that encourage informal ad hoc small group conversation, (7) recognize the tendency that while standing, people tend to cluster in the center of an open space and/or in traffic lanes, but while seated they prefer to be on the edge of the room, (8) accept the fact that women prefer slightly more space between one another than do men, (9) plan one low-key activity every week in one corner of an adjacent room that will attract and interest younger children, (10) define a corner with its own beverage table for teenagers, (11) provide an occasional opportunity for upcoming special programs or events to be publicized, and (12) perhaps use another wall for a three- or four-week exhibit by a painter or photographer or weaver.

In other words, if that fellowship period fails on its own to attract a satisfactory number of participants, ask someone to accept responsibility for making it a planned and attractive event that will encourage people to return next week.

The third common problem with the fellowship period is a result of the differences in the size of congregations. In the congregation with fewer than a hundred at worship, it may be adequate to simply announce it and provide the refreshments. Most of the people will come.

In the middle-sized congregations that average between one hundred and two hundred at Sunday morning worship, only one-half of the attenders may participate in the fellowship period. Usually it will be necessary to plan it more carefully and to have someone in charge of the design for the week, as well as someone else responsible for the refreshments, to increase that number of participants.

In the big congregation the fellowship period rarely attracts a majority of the attenders unless either (a) it is held in a room through which nearly everyone passes to enter or leave the sanctuary, and/or (b) every week is a carefully planned event with a variety of attractive features—and that means someone in charge with additional volunteer assistance.

Finally, three comments should be made about the factor

of the time zone. First, as a general rule, the farther west one travels on this continent, the more likely that people will be going to church earlier. In North Carolina or Georgia, the general pattern appears to be that people prefer to begin Sunday morning worship at ten-thirty or eleven while in California scores of large congregations have their largest attendance at the eight-thirty or nine o'clock service.

Second, the National Football League games and other television programs make it more difficult for churches in the West to keep people past eleven-thirty on Sunday morning than is the case in the East.

Third, churches located in the eastern end of any time zone usually find people more responsive to an early hour in the winter than do congregations in the western end of the same time zone. Thus, the congregation meeting in the eastern end of a time zone east of the Mississippi may find people willing to linger for the fellowship period after worship (except in the Southeast where a high priority is to beat the Methodists or the Baptists to the cafeteria) while in Kansas, Nebraska, the Dakotas, and the Pacific Coast it may be wise to plan a much earlier fellowship period.

A critical point, which many church leaders find to be repugnant, is that in addition to all the good reasons to design an attractive fellowship period on Sunday morning, one additional benefit of the fellowship time is that it does increase attendance.

More than a dozen years after his arrival as the new senior minister at First Church, Pastor Don Johnson experienced an intense period of self-examination accompanied by considerable ambivalence. By that time the average attendance at Sunday morning worship had plateaued at approximately nine hundred, the shortage of available parking made it clear to Don that was probably the ceiling. As he reflected back on his years at First Church, he began to regret he had insisted on the renovation of the fellowship hall and that entire capital improvements program. In retrospect it was clear to him that a wise and farsighted leader would have urged the congregation to relocate to a ten-, fifteen-, or twenty-acre site and construct new facilities that would take into account the new realities of life that include the disappearance of the geographical parish, the increased dependence on the private automobile, the demand for diversified programming that can be offered only by a very large congregation, the erosion of denominational loyalties, the demand for higher quality facilities for places of public assemblage and the fear of crime.[2] In retrospect, Don was right. It probably would have been better if First Church had relocated many years earlier. The fact of the matter was that if Don had proposed relocation and stuck to that position, he probably would have served a brief pastorate as Dr. Bennington's unintentional interim successor.

One evening as Don discussed his reflections and raised questions about his own leadership with Mary, she reminded him, "Remember, Honey, the call is to be faithful and obedient, not to be right or wise or successful. You've been both faithful and obedient and that's all God asks of you." In this context, Mary was right and Don was wrong.

Frustrations and Questions

Chapter Seven

"Don, you've been at First Church for nearly ten years now, what's the biggest frustration you experienced as a senior minister?" asked Ted Stevens, the driver of the car carrying Don and two other senior ministers to a two-day university-sponsored seminar on pastoral counseling.

"That's an easy question," replied Don. "During my first fifteen years in the ministry, when I was serving smaller congregations, I was convinced I knew practically all my people, and I felt I knew most of them better than they knew me. Now we have a large number of people at First Church who know me better than I know them. That makes it harder for me to carry on a conversation when I meet one of the members on the street. Occasionally people will greet me like a close friend, and I can't even call them by name."

Don is describing what has been called "the President Roosevelt syndrome." Back in the 1930s, when he was making those fireside chats to the nation over the radio, Franklin D. Roosevelt became the close friend of millions, most of whom he had never met. The same phenomenon is now encountered by television personalities such as Johnny Carson, Robert Schuller, Dan Rather, and Ted Koppel as well as scores of senior ministers. On a more limited scale that same relationship is encountered by high school teachers, mayors, bishops, university professors, and pastors serving large congregations. They become the focal point of a large group, and members become very knowledgeable about the leader. It is impossible for the leader to become that knowledgeable about that many different people.

"My biggest frustration is the churches and theological seminaries spend a lot of time teaching ministers how to begin a new pastorate. There must be two dozen books in print on that one subject, but no one teaches us how to terminate a pastorate," grumbled Kern Miller, the oldest person in the car. "I've followed two senior pastors and neither one knew how to leave gracefully. The one who retired and stayed in the community was willing to give up the preaching and administration, but it took three years before he would surrender his pastoral care responsibilities. He wanted to continue making pastoral calls, burying the dead, and officiating at weddings. The other simply left a mountain of unfinished business and incomplete records. It appears he assumed the church would close the day after he left."[1]

The reason these four senior ministers were together is that each, unknown to the other three, had signed up for this overnight continuing education event. When the sponsoring university had mailed out the final details on the event, a list of all registrants was included. Don, to his surprise, had discovered three others were from his city. The only one he could call a close friend was Ted Stevens, who offered to drive if Don would contact the other two.

One of the other two was Kern Miller, the senior minister of a twenty-seven-year-old, very large, and theologically conservative congregation that met in a building on a twenty-acre site on the east edge of the city. Don had never met Pastor Miller, but he had seen him on television dozens of times and had no difficulty recognizing him when they met at Ted's church early that Tuesday morning.

The fourth was the only Anglo woman in the county who was the senior minister of a large congregation affiliated with one of the old-line Protestant denominations. Don had met Ruth Douglas on three or four previous occasions but her church was of a different denomination and located on the other side of the city a good twelve miles distant from First Church.

"My number-one frustration is not really related so much

to being a senior minister as to the ministry in more general terms," reflected Ted Stevens. "This is the ethical issue of encouraging a pastor to move on to some other church after messing up in one or two churches. For example, I followed a minister who was forced to leave after it was discovered he was sleeping with two or three women in the congregation. He moved to another state and the same thing happened again. He's now serving a church in a different denomination. There should be some way to get rid of guys like that after one episode."

"I suppose the libel laws and the possibility of being sued for defamation of character scares some denominational leaders or else they believe everyone deserves a second chance," commented Ruth Douglas, "but I expect most of us know what you're talking about."

"Related to that is another issue," declared Kern Miller. "How do you get preachers to leave when most of their support has disappeared? Our church has a constitution that requires a two-thirds favorable vote at a congregational meeting before a minister can be called, but the same paragraph also requires a two-thirds vote by the congregation to terminate the call. That means a candidate with 65 percent support cannot be called, but after you've been called, you can stay if you have only 35 percent support."

"My biggest point of frustration is one that none of you fellows experience," declared Ruth Douglas. "Two years ago I came as the first woman to be a senior minister in our denomination in this state. My predecessor, who was a man and also a real gentleman, did everything anyone could possibly ask to prepare the way for me before he retired. Five years earlier, when the associate minister left, he pioneered in bringing a woman on the staff as his associate. I've never met her, but apparently she was very competent. She left a few months before he did, and he insisted the position be left vacant so his successor could have a voice in filling it. About a year and a half ago we filled that vacancy with a capable young man who is about twenty years younger than I. He's doing a great job, but I rarely hear anyone make reference to gender as a factor in why he does what he does or why he excels in certain aspects of ministry and may be a little deficient in some other areas. Many of the comments I hear about my performance as the new minister, both good and bad, have a gender reference attached to them as though that explains everything I do or why I do it that way. When our secretary retired after thirty-five years, the first question I was asked about a successor was whether I preferred a male or female secretary."

"One of my biggest frustrations which I hadn't thought about until we started this conversation," added Don, "is that I have about two dozen highly competent lay leaders who are convinced the concept of economy of scale should apply to big churches. They insist that our unit costs, as they define them, should be lower because a big church should be able to achieve economies not available to the small churches. We've more than doubled our worship attendance, but after you allow for inflation, our expenditures have tripled and some of our people can't understand this."

"I hear that same garbage," added Ted Stevens, "and so I checked into it. That was a red hot subject back in the 1950s and 1960s, but the idea of economy of scale has been largely discredited during the past twenty years when it comes to person-centered services. It still applies to the production of goods, but not the production of person-centered services. It doesn't matter whether you compare the cost of a police department in a large city and a small town or the cost of running a large hospital versus a small one. Unit costs go up because as the size of the organization increases, people expect both more services and higher quality."

"That's good to hear," noted Don. "Maybe I can use that to help explain to our malcontents why we're now spending so much on our music program. We've raised the quality and also greatly increased the participation."

"As a general rule," explained Kern Miller, "per-person expenditures in a large church are three to six times what they are in a smaller congregation. The key point to remember is the distinction between costs and expenditures. The cost of a sermon, on a per person in the room basis, may be only one-fifth as much in the big church as it is in a smaller one, but the big church has many expenditures the small ones never make."

"Another gripe I have is this increasing emphasis on hiring part-time staff people because that's a cheaper way to build a staff than with full-time people," declared Ted Stevens in a tone of voice that suggested this may be his biggest point of frustration. "I've tried it and it hasn't worked for me. It's almost impossible to schedule staff meetings when everyone can be there, and a couple have been so emotionally tied to their full-time jobs they're worn out when they show up at the church."

"We have five part-time program staff people and I'm delighted with four of the five," commented Ruth Douglas. "As I've listened to other senior ministers complain about their part-time help, I've asked myself why we're so lucky. One reason is that none of our part-time people have any other employment. This is their only job. One is retired and three are homemakers. Second, each one has only one basic assignment. Each is a specialist. I'm not sure whether I would want a part-time generalist. Being a specialist enables them to be at the top of their own ladder in terms of status. Our part-time organist is by far the best organist in our congregation. Our part-time parish visitor has been on the staff ever since he took early retirement eight years ago, and he knows more about our members than anyone else. Our number-one success story is a woman we pay $6,000 a year to concentrate on the assimilation of new members, and everyone agrees she is doing a superb job. The part-time director of our three-day-a-week preschool program is our expert on early childhood development. I'm convinced the best program staff is one in which every person is at the top of the status ladder in his or her specialty. My associate, who is full-time, is the most competent minister in our conference in the field of adult education. The one place we have problems is in music. We have a part-time choir director who is clearly over the hill, but she has only two years to go to retirement and no one is willing to face the issue. She is the only unhappy person we have in the program staff and I'm convinced she's unhappy because of her lack of competence in her speciality."[2]

"It helps if every part-time staff person knows clearly the expectations the church has for that person, if the goals are precisely defined, and if the reward system is consistent," added Don, "but I think there is a limit on what you should expect of part-time staff people in terms of relationships with the rest of the staff. The best part-time staff I've worked with have been more goal-oriented than relational. Their focus is on ministry and performance, not staff relationships."

"Maybe my expectations have been unrealistic," conceded the driver, "but I still place a great emphasis on building a compatible and harmonious staff team."

"It also helps to remember there is a big difference between the people who really thrive while they are working at two or three different jobs and whether or not each of those employers thrive," noted Ruth who was happy with her part-time staffers. "It's true some employers exploit their employees, but it also is true some employees exploit their employer."

"I guess none of you may have this problem," observed Kern, "but one of the frustrations I feel is that in our denomination the moderator is a very influential person for that one year. In our church the senior minister, the moderator, and the vice-moderator, who is expected to move up to moderator the following year, constitute a troika. Our people see the job of moderator more as a ceremonial position that should be a reward for long years of meritorious service. In fact it is a key position. When I came nineteen years ago, that troika was composed of the senior minister, the moderator, and the person who had been the moderator the previous year. After five years I got that changed because it created a past orientation. I wanted the third person to be next year's moderator and thus build in more of a future orientation. The choice of the moderator pretty much determines whether I'll have a good year or a bad year. Our best moderators have been newer members who have had lots of experience as a volunteer in the church before moving here.

"While I'm old enough to know better," continued Kern, "I guess another one of my points of frustration, or maybe it's really guilt, surfaces when I hear senior ministers talk about how hard they work, how many hours they put in every week, and how they stay on top of every detail. I'm sixty-three years old. I've been in this church for nineteen years and I'm convinced I now have more discretionary time than I've ever had before. We have nine full-time ministers on our staff, plus six full-time laypeople and a bunch of part-time people. We have an executive minister who takes care of most of the administration and supervises the office and custodial staff. Our program director runs the program. I preach forty-five Sundays a year, take my turn going to the hospitals three or four days a week, call on prospective new members, and do a few other things. I have my share of funerals and weddings, but less than a third of them. I think I average ten to fifteen hours a week for study, discretionary reading, and other things. My wife and I take a week off right after Easter, three weeks in the summer, and the first two weeks of January. We have a good staff and maybe I'm wrong to let them do so much, but we're averaging nearly 1,600 at worship now compared to less than 300 when I came nineteen years ago. We have eight grandchildren and I see every one of them at least four or five times a year. I also play golf once or twice a week all summer."

"I guess you know your priorities, and you know how to delegate," observed Don Johnson with a combination of envy and admiration. It also should have been apparent to everyone in the car that Kern Miller had drastically understated his own work load. In addition to his role as a local television personality, Pastor Miller also represented the community image of that large congregation. He was a strong and wise leader with a clearly defined set of priorities, and he knew how to earn the loyalty of his staff, both paid and volunteer. Only on the return trip did Kern's colleagues discover his formal education ended after one year of college.

"Let me raise one more issue with you guys that really troubles me," said Ruth Douglas. "I was very active as a lay volunteer in the church for years before I went to seminary and for at least thirty years I've been told the people have to own the plans before you try to implement those plans. How do you get the people to own the vision? Our church has a governing board of forty-five people and I'd be dead and forgotten if I waited for every one of them to feel a sense of ownership before we went ahead and implemented new ideas. We're getting a lot done, but we surely don't have broad based ownership for most of it."

"You've just raised three important points if you want to be a happy senior minister," declared her sixty-three-year-old companion, Kern Miller, who was seated next to her in the rear seat of the car and who, a few minutes earlier, had complained about how extremely busy pastors made him feel guilty about having so much discretionary time. "First of all, don't let other people make you feel guilty. Too many preachers spend too much time either making themselves feel guilty about what they're not doing or letting other people make them feel guilty. That's not productive.

"Second," he continued, "don't try to be overly consistent. There are times when you need broad based support, but in a big church, unlike in a small congregation, those occasions are few and far between.

"Third, this business of broad based ownership of goals oversimplifies a complex issue and neglects the difference between ownership and support," continued this experienced senior minister who comes from a tradition that does not ordain women, but who was clearly impressed with the competence of his new friend. "While my church is three times the size of yours, you have to remember you are the senior minister of a big church. My guess is that in your church, which you said has eight hundred members, you need about 1 percent of your members to feel a sense of ownership of that vision, maybe 5 percent who will be active supporters, another 20 percent who can be persuaded to approve it, and perhaps a fourth who can be talked into going along. The other half are folks who can be ignored. They won't help you and they won't fight you."

This conversation raises five of the crucial distinctions between the small church and the large multiple-staff congregation.

The basic generalization is that the larger the congregation, the smaller the percentage of members who need to feel at least some degree of ownership of a proposal for change. In the really small church that figure may be 40 percent. In the 100-member congregation it may be 10 percent, in the

200-member church it may be 8 percent, while in the 500-member church it probably is no more than 2 or 3 percent.

The second generalization is that the larger the number of members, the greater the need for inspiration or challenging or motivating leadership and the less the emphasis on participatory democracy. It is close to impossible to make a carefully thought-out policy decision at a meeting attended by four hundred people.

The third generalization is that in the large multiple-staff congregation enlisting complete support from every member of the program staff is more important than securing unanimous approval from that big governing board.

The fourth generalization, which overlaps the first three, is that as the size of the membership figure goes up, the quality of support becomes more important than the quantity. A few highly committed, competent, and active workers are far more valuable than a couple of hundred passive supporters.

Finally, the larger the size of the congregation, the more critical it is to build an effective internal reporting system so people know what is happening and why little time should be spent on worrying about broad based ownership of every program proposal. In the small congregation asking permission and/or winning support is an effective means of perpetuating tribal customs, reinforcing continuity, keeping the newcomers from seizing control, minimizing change, maintaining harmony with the congregational culture, and enhancing the feeling of lay control. By contrast, in the large church, the senior minister recognizes that in a crisis it is easier to win forgiveness than it is to get advance permission, that the withholding of disapproval may be as important as winning approval, and that performance rather than continuity or majority support is the key yardstick in how members evaluate what is happening.

"I must confess I was overwhelmed when you said your staff includes nine ministers, plus six full-time laypeople," remarked Ruth to Kern Miller. "Are those six laypeople your secretarial staff?"

"Nope," replied Kern. "Those are all program staff. We

also have about eight or nine secretaries, bookkeepers, and computer operators, plus five custodians."

"That must be nice to be in a big church where you can afford such a huge staff," interrupted Ted in an obviously envious tone of voice. "We could never afford that many staff people in our church."

"You got it backward," declared Kern. "The reason we have such a big staff is not because we're a big church. The reason we average over 1,600 at worship when we have fewer than a thousand members is that we have a big staff of highly competent people. The competence and the size of the staff comes first; it is not simply a product of size."

"Which seminary is your number-one source for your ministerial staff?" inquired the fifty-three-year-old Ruth Douglas, who was getting acquainted with a type of ministry she had never encountered before. Up until today she had been proud of the fact that her 800-member congregation averaged 450 at worship, a ratio far above the average for big churches in her denomination.

"Years ago I tried to recruit from our two seminaries," answered Kern, "but I finally decided that wasn't working. Eight of the nine ministers on our staff today are men who first met Jesus Christ through our ministry. After they accepted Christ as their personal Savior and joined our church, they became active workers. Later we lifted them up to volunteer leadership positions. When each of these eight came to me to talk about his call to the ministry, I subsequently asked him to come on our staff. After they came on staff, we arranged for them to go to school on a part-time basis."

"Where did they go to school?" asked Ruth.

"We've arranged with two seminaries to use our church as an extension center," continued Kern. "We have people coming from a hundred-mile radius to take classes on our campus. None of our eight ministers spent as much as a full year on a seminary campus. Each one did almost all of his classroom work at our church. Although I've never been to seminary myself, I want all of my ministerial staff to have a seminary education, but I really am not interested in their getting the socialization experience you get by living on a seminary campus for three years. I want them to understand, value, and support the values our church believes in and teaches."

"You want your staff to be socialized into the culture of your congregation, not your denomination, if I hear you correctly?" questioned Ruth.

"Not exactly," commented Kern. "A good many of us are not exactly convinced that either of our seminaries really prepares people to fit into the churches of our brotherhood. We believe seminaries really prepare people for going on to graduate school, not for pastoral ministry."

"Did I hear you say that every person in your congregation who felt a call to the ministry ended up on your staff?" asked Ted.

"Oh, no," quickly replied Kern. "More than thirty of our members have received a call from God to go into the ministry or to go into the mission field. I felt these eight had the gifts and skills we needed on our staff. My executive minister was running his own business with over seven hundred employees when he finally responded to the Lord's call. Our minister of education was an elementary school principal when he decided his real call was to the ordained ministry. Our minister of evangelism had been selling insurance for over thirty years when he answered his call to ministry. Our minister of health had been a nurse in the Marine Corps, was discharged, and worked in the local hospital for several years before going into the ministry. Our minister of parish life had spent nearly twenty years as the agricultural agent in Washington County when he came on staff."

"Where did you find those six lay program staff members?" inquired Ted.

"Same thing," explained Kern. "We lifted them up from among our members. We invited them to give up their secular jobs and come work for us. Everyone took a cut in pay to do that."

"Sounds as if you're building an inbred organization where everyone has to walk the party line," observed Ted Stevens who held four earned academic degrees.

"That may be true," conceded Kern, "but we average about

1,600 on Sunday morning. I don't think I heard you say what your attendance is."

Kern Miller was describing three of the most significant trends of the last quarter of the twentieth century. One is the increasing number of seminaries offering classes off campus, often in church buildings. This trend may have its greatest visibility in California, but it has spread to all parts of the continent. It no longer is necessary to go to a seminary campus to earn a seminary degree.

A second is the growing trend among large churches to recruit staff from among the members rather than to turn to theological seminaries for program staff.

The third trend overlaps the first two. For several generations fledgling ministers were trained by pastors. The next stage was the creation of theological seminaries to train pastors. More recently scores of large churches have become the primary training centers for future program staff members, both lay and ordained.

"What's the biggest change you've experienced in doing ministry?" asked Don who decided that with over one hundred miles yet to go the time had come to change the subject.

"That's easy," observed Ruth Douglas very quickly. "Thirty-five years ago when I was in high school the idea of a woman becoming a minister was not on the list of possibilities. Now we have women serving as bishops, conference ministers, district superintendents, presbytery executives, and in other positions that no one even discussed thirty years ago."

"I think the most significant change in recent years is illustrated by this trip," suggested Ted Stevens. "Here we are, four senior ministers from four widely different denominational backgrounds going off to a continuing education event sponsored by a state university. It used to be either the seminaries or the denomination sponsored all the continuing education events a pastor needed. Now more and more are being offered by para-church organizations or public agencies or nondenominational retreat centers or by individual churches."

"I think it's a more complicated issue than simply

continuing education," offered Don. "Last August I attended a special event for senior ministers held in a big church in Minnesota. We had people from a dozen denominations in the group. The one common thread I heard for three days was alienation from the denomination."

"That's part of it," agreed Ted. "I used to go to our regional convention every year plus several other denominational events. About a year after I became a senior minister, I cut that out of my schedule. Now I show up at our regional convention for a day or so. Their agenda has about zero overlap with mine, so I don't bother going, and I no longer serve on any denominational committees."

"The biggest change I've seen," reflected the sixty-three-year-old Kern Miller, "is that today most of the independent churches are either theologically very conservative or fundamentalist. I can remember back in the 1950s when nearly every big city had at least one or two strong independent churches that were at the far liberal end of the theological spectrum."

"That reflects the general swing of the theological pendulum, doesn't it?" asked Don. "Isn't that swing to the theological right why your congregation is five times as big as it was when you arrived on the scene?"

"Along with that has been the big increase in the number of Asian and Spanish language congregations," commented Ruth Douglas. "My understanding is that most of the Asian congregations are quite conservative theologically."

"I'm not so sure that is the distinctive characteristic of the Asian churches," observed Ted Stevens. "I think the number-one reason behind the emergence of what must be thousands of new Asian congregations is that the church is at the very center of life for many of the immigrants from the Pacific Rim. We Anglos want them to join our Anglo churches to relieve our guilt by proving we are inclusive congregations, but we can't offer what they are looking for, which is to be part of a caring group that has a high degree of homogeneity. You can see the same dynamic at work if you study the first immigrants to this country from Germany, Poland, Scandinavia, Italy, and Central Europe. Their churches also were the center of their life in a new world."

"One of the biggest changes I've experienced in my years in the ministry," observed Don, "is the change in the sources of our money to finance the church. When I first entered the ministry, we just assumed you financed the church out of the offering plate. We asked our members to give out of their current income and they did. Our treasurer told me the other day that this year at First Church we will receive 8 percent of our total receipts from the income from our endowment fund, which is a form of accumulated wealth, 14 percent from user fees, 3 percent from a variety of money-raising activities, 2 percent from memorial gifts, at least 5 percent from contributions from people who are not on the membership roll, and close to 20 percent in designated second-mile giving, over half of which goes for missions."

"That means less than half of your total income will come from the regular giving of today's members," marveled Ted Stevens who had been adding up the percentages as Don spoke. "Doesn't that put you in a pretty shaky financial position?"

"I certainly hope not!" declared Ruth Douglas. "While our budget is nowhere near as big as what you have at First Church, Don, the combination of income from the endowment fund, special appeals, and user fees account for close to 60 percent of our total income. The fees for our weekday preschool program and Mothers' Day Out amount to over a fourth of our current income."

"Let me ask you about another change I've seen," continued this fifty-three-year-old grandmother who had celebrated her thirty-eighth birthday before graduating from college and was a forty-year-old widow when she entered seminary. "As I told you earlier, I've spent far more years as a lay volunteer in the church than I have as an ordained minister, and one of the big changes I think I've seen is this huge increase in weekday Bible study groups for both men and women, but especially women."

"When I arrived nineteen years ago," added Kern Miller, "we had three Bible study groups that met during the week, two for women and one for men. Their combined attendance for an average week was less than sixty. Now we have over nine hundred women meeting in Bible study groups every week and at least a third of those nine hundred women do not come from our congregation."

"Where do they come from?" inquired Ted.

"From your congregations, Don's church, and probably close to fifty or sixty other churches. If you don't offer what they want people will keep looking until they find it."

At this Ted Stevens began to contemplate the joys of driving to meetings with no one in the back seat of the car.

"Another change that is a recent one and I must admit I haven't caught up with it myself, but our church has," interjected Ruth, relieved that Kern had not mentioned her church as a source of members for his women's Bible study classes. "That's the computer. We now have all of our membership and financial records in the computer, and we've replaced all our typewriters with word processors. My secretary really knows the system and she can answer about any question I ask. The word processor also has greatly increased her productivity."

"It is a great tool," agreed Kern. "I have my own personal computer and it's great for sermon preparation. I don't know anything about how they operate, but one of my members gave me a file program and taught me how to use it. Now I can punch in anything I want that deals with Palm Sunday, for example. If I read something in a book or a magazine or a commentary on Palm Sunday, I make a refernce to it in the computer. When I get ready to prepare my sermon, the computer lifts up all those references for me. I do the same thing with topics such as conversion or Advent or heaven or suicide or baptism or a couple of hundred other topics. It surely beats those file folders I used for so many years."

"How much storage capacity do you have?" inquired Ted.

"I haven't the faintest idea," declared Kern, "but apparently I have enough. It's still working."

"Another change I've seen that bothers me," reflected Don, "is how the spoken word has replaced the written word. Today I write far fewer letters, but I make a lot more telephone calls than I did when I first entered the ministry."

"That's true," agreed Ted. "Today when I make a reference during a sermon on what was reported on television, everyone nods agreement, but if I make a reference to what I read in a magazine or a book, I get a lot of blank stares."

"Don't overlook the power of the written word," advised Ruth. "I still mail fifteen to twenty handwritten notes every day to reach people on their birthday or wedding anniversary or some other important occasion. Today my secretary will mail about fifteen and before leaving, I wrote another three dozen, some of which are to be mailed tomorrow and the rest the day after tomorrow."

"Your members receive your pastoral care even when you're out of town," commented Kern admiringly. "I think I better start doing that when we get back."

"Let me try one on you," said Ted. "One of the biggest changes I've seen during the past fifteen years is that I now have lots of memorial services without the body being present. Last year we kept track and my associate and I had a combined total of twenty-three funerals. At nine of those services there was no casket in the room. In four the body had been cremated and in the other five burial was scheduled for another day at a considerable distance from our church."

"While I only had about a dozen funerals last year," reflected Ruth, "my experience was similar. Cremations now are far more common than they used to be."

"That's not my experience at all," observed Kern. "Our people still want the body at the service. The only difference I see when I compare today with thirty-five years ago is that now the casket usually is closed. It used to always be open and everyone would parade by the casket before it was closed."

"Let me change the subject and I would like to go back to how you pick people for your staff," suggested Ruth Douglas. "We're getting ready to look for another part-time program staff person. What do you fellows ask when you interview candidates?"

"The first questions I ask are about their call," quickly replied Kern. "I don't want anyone unless he is convinced he has a clear and unambiguous call from God to be in the parish ministry. I don't pretend to know whom God calls, all I know is who responds. At times I believe the number who respond may be greater than the number who have a genuine call."

"We turned down two candidates for our vacancy for an

associate minister a couple of years ago," commented Ted, "when it turned out their real concern was not to come and join our staff, but to get out of where they were. I really probe to find out why they want to leave where they are. Of course I also want to know why they want to come on our staff. Our denomination has a surplus of clergy so we can be choosy when we look for a new associate."

"I ask about gifts, skills, and competence," observed Don. "I want to know what they do best. If the answer is one-to-one relationships with people, that takes care of that. I want people who excel in working with groups of people, not one-to-one relationships. I also want people who have a specialized competence in some area of ministry or program."

"That may explain what you said earlier about your experience with part-time program staff people," reflected Ruth. "You told us awhile back that you had found part-time program staff people to be primarily task-oriented rather than strongly relational. Could it be that is your experience because that's what you seek?"

"Could be," admitted Don, "but my experience tells me you can divide all associate ministers into four categories. One group is composed of those who see serving on the staff of a large church as one step on the ministerial ladder. Another group is composed, as Ted said a minute ago, of people who need to leave where they are or who choose to be an associate minister while they test out their call to the parish ministry or simply need a place to land. A third group is composed of those who see the staff of a large church as a mutual support group and who want to be part of a team ministry, rather than be out on their own. The fourth group is composed of people who want to concentrate their energies on fulfilling the ministry goals of the congregation they're serving. I want to build my staff completely out of people from this fourth group."

"Those aren't mutually exclusive categories," objected Ruth Douglas, "and they don't cover all associate ministers. My associate is an exceptionally competent specialist who feels a calling to be a career associate minister, but he also wants to be part of a supportive team. He fits your third and fourth categories to some extent, but really represents a distinctively different category than what you've described."

"I have another question I picked up from a Southern Baptist minister in Amarillo," interjected Kern. "I tell those who join our staff we have two immediate expectations of them. One is to buy a house and the other is to buy a cemetery lot. That takes care of Don's first two categories. We want people who expect to stay until they die. If they want a housing allowance so they can rent, I have a lot less interest in them."

"I'm a widow, and my kids are all grown," explained Ruth as she introduced a new topic, "but I'm curious about how you men make time for your families."

"I'll tell you what I do," volunteered Ted Stevens. "Both of our kids are in college and my wife has a good job, but she rarely gets home before six. So on five days a week, and everybody in my congregation knows this so if they have to get a hold of me, they know to call our house, I go home at four o'clock to cook dinner for my wife and me. When she walks in the door at six o'clock, I will have prepared a delicious meal and I also will have completed my mental rehearsal for whatever meeting I'm going to that night. If I don't have a committee meeting that evening, I work on my sermon. I do my best thinking while I'm preparing a meal. Somehow that seems to get my creative juices flowing. One out of five days I work on a sermon that I can have completely outlined in my head by the time my wife gets home. During the typical week I will spend a couple of those two-hour blocks of time preparing for a meeting, one or two working on a sermon, which I may not preach for another month or two, and one out of five I will work out in my head the final details for the next morning's staff meeting or develop the central organizing principle for a new adult group we need to organize or outline the column I write for our weekly newsletter or prepare a report I have to write. Ten minutes after my wife walks in the door, I have the meal on the table."

"Sounds to me as if you're always working on church business, even when you are cooking a meal," said Ruth. "Do you go over those mental outlines with your wife while you eat?"

"Nope!" replied Ted sharply. "We spend at least the first half of the time at the table on her day and on what happened to her that day. I try not to let church business interfere with my home life."

That last comment brought a roar of laughter from the other three.

"I told you earlier," explained Kern, "that my wife and I spend six weeks every year traveling together, and we don't neglect our grandchildren."

"Let me go back to your earlier question, Ruth, about choosing a staff," interrupted Don. "Maybe my four categories do oversimplify the world, but let me risk an even greater oversimplification. It seems to me that in staffing a large church you can go down one of two roads. One is primarily concerned with the needs and the agenda of the individual staff members. The other is to place the primary focus on the congregation and on outreach beyond the membership. I want to focus on that second road in building my staff."

"I think you have to be concerned with both," argued Ruth. "It's not an either-or choice."

"That's why I used the word primary. I want the primary focus to be on doing ministry and the secondary emphasis to be on the needs of the individual staff members. Perhaps my use of four categories was too simple, but my point was that I don't want to build a staff in response to the needs of the individual staff members, I want to build a staff around doing ministry."

"You guys sure are goal-oriented," declared Ruth. "That may be why we don't look at the world the same way. I still haven't figured out whether Ted cooks dinner five nights a week to make life easier for his wife or to create an environment for him to do his creative thinking."

"This traveling seminar is about to take a twenty-seven-hour recess," declared Ted as he drove into the parking lot of the university's center for continuing education.

"Well, I certainly have enjoyed it," Kern said in a warm and gracious tone, "and this has been a great educational experience for me just getting acquainted with you three."

"This has been the best instruction on being a senior minister I've had since I became one two years ago," added Ruth. "You three have been superb teachers for the past few hours, and I look forward to the advanced course on the way home."

"Yep, being with you three sure beats reading a book about being a senior minister," agreed Ted as he crawled out of the driver's seat and locked the car.

Notes

Chapter One

1 For suggestions on how a congregation chooses a new minister and how a pastor picks a new parish see Lyle E. Schaller, *The Pastor and the People,* rev. ed. (Nashville: Abingdon Press, 1986), pp. 19-55.

2. For varying expectations the members place on the pastor see Lyle E. Schaller, *Looking in the Mirror* (Nashville: Abingdon Press, 1984), pp. 14-37.

3. An extensive description of the passive church is in Lyle E. Schaller, *Activating the Passive Church* (Nashville: Abingdon Press, 1981), pp. 40-70.

4. For the value of special Sundays see Lyle E. Schaller and Edward Lee Tucker, *44 Ways to Increase Church Attendance* (Nashville: Abingdon Press, 1988), chapter 1.

Chapter Two

1. Samuel Kernell and Samuel L. Popkin, ed. *Chief of Staff: Twenty-five Years of Managing the Presidency* (Berkeley: University of California Press, 1986).

2. A useful book on the family as one model of staff relationships is Paula Bernstein, *Family Ties, Corporate Bonds* (New York: Doubleday, 1985). Another that speaks to the process and dynamics of family models in the church is Edwin H. Friedman, *Generation to Generation* (New York: The Guilford Press, 1985). A classic in this field is Augustus Y. Napier and Carl A. Whitaker, *The Family Crucible* (New York: Bantam Books, 1980).

3. Although this is offered only as a piece of speculation for someone else to research, during the past dozen years this writer has asked more than a thousand ministers, "Who reared you? Your mother? Your father? Or this question doesn't fit your background?" The majority of ministers identify their mother. The vast majority of pastors, both male and female, serving small churches or as associate pastors in large churches also identify their mother as the person who reared them. A slight majority of the senior ministers of large congregations who respond identify their father, about a fourth identify their mother, and the rest pick the third option. This sample may not be representative.

4. Reported in James Rhem, "Bad Blood in Academia," *Isthmus of Madison* (Wisconsin), June 29–July 5, 1984, vol. 9, 26, pp. 1, 8-11. In looking at the corporate world, Blotnick found that in two out of five cases the mentor dismissed the protégé within three years. Srully Blotnick, *The Corporate Steeplechase: Predictable Crises in a Business Career* (New York: Facts on File, 1984).

5. An excellent book on this subject is Seymour B. Sarason, *The Creation of Settings and the Future Societies* (San Francisco: Jossey-Bass, Publishers, 1972).

6. For reflections on this distinction see Abraham Zalezink, "Managers and Leaders: Are They Different?" in *Executive Success: Making It in Management*, ed. Eliza G. C. Collins (New York: John Wiley & Sons, 1983), pp. 123-39; Warren Bennis and Burt Nanus, *Leaders: The Strategies of Taking Charge* (New York: Harper & Row, 1985); and Lyle E. Schaller, *Getting Things Done* (Nashville: Abingdon Press, 1986).

7. When the military academies admitted women as cadets for the first time each of the four studied both the process and the results. The best is Judith Hicks Stiehm, *Bring Me Men and Women: Mandated Changes at the U.S. Air Force Academy* (Berkeley: University of California Press, 1981).

8. An excellent statement on feminist theory and political action with an extensive bibliography is Diane L. Fowlkes, "Feminist Theory—Reconstructing Research and Teaching About American Politics and Government," in *News for Teachers of Political Science* (Washington, D.C.: American Political Science Association, 1987), 82, pp. 6-9.

9. An example of the shift from a predominantly male staff in a large church to a largely female staff is described in Lyle E. Schaller, *It's a Different World!* (Nashville: Abingdon Press, 1987), pp. 200-208.

10. Quoted in "Managing the Woman's Way," *Newsweek*, March 17, 1986, pp. 46-47. See also Marilyn Loden, *Feminine Leadership, or How to Succeed in Business Without Being One of the Boys* (New York: Times Books, 1985).

11. For an elaboration of this largely neglected point see Peter Drucker, "How to Manage the Boss," *The Wall Street Journal*, August 1, 1986.

12. See Lyle E. Schaller, "Why Not a Minister of Health?" *Church Management—The Clergy Journal*, January 1985.

13. For two provocative accounts of how ministry is formed in the church, not in the seminary, see Janet F. Fishburn and Neill Q. Hamilton, "Seminary Education Tested by Praxis," *The Christian Century*, February 1-8, 1984, pp. 108-12, and Jack E. Weller and M. Anderson Sale, "Students Speak Out; Presbytery Responds," *The Christian Century*, April 22, 1987, pp. 384-85.

14. For a brief introduction into the complexity of this issue see "Variety of Diaconate Bewildering," *The Lutheran*, May 6, 1987, p. 18.

15. A lucid introduction to the Myers-Briggs Type Indicator (MBTI) is Thomas Moore, "Personality Tests Are Back," *Fortune*, March 30, 1987, pp. 74-82.

Chapter Three

1. For suggestions on moving from vocal choirs to a broader music program and for building a large choir see Lyle E. Schaller, "Music in the Large Church," *Choristers Guild Letters*, March 1980, pp. 123-25; "Choirs or Music Program," *Choristers Guild Letters*, May 1984, pp. 185-87; "How Large Is Your Choir?" *Choristers Guild Letters*, January 1985, pp. 83-85.

2. For an extended discussion of why internal adversary relationships within a congregation tend to be detrimental see Lyle E. Schaller, *Looking in the Mirror* (Nashville: Abingdon Press, 1984), pp. 38-58.

Chapter Five

1. Peter Drucker, "Getting Things Done: How to Make People Decisions," *Harvard Business Review,* July–August 1985, pp. 22-26.

2. For an extensive discussion of the dynamics of large groups see Lyle E. Schaller, *Effective Church Planning* (Nashville: Abingdon Press, 1979), pp. 17-63.

3. See Warren J. Hartman, *Five Audiences* (Nashville: Abingdon Press, 1987), and Dick Murray, *Strengthening the Adult Sunday School Class* (Nashville: Abingdon Press, 1981).

4. James W. Fowler, *Stages of Faith* (New York: Harper & Row, 1981) and Mary M. Wilcox, *Developmental Journey* (Nashville: Abingdon Press, 1979).

5. Dick Murray, *Teaching the Bible to Adults and Youth* (Nashville: Abingdon Press, 1987).

Chapter Six

1. For additional suggestions on increasing attendance see Lyle E. Schaller and Edward Lee Tucker, *44 Ways to Increase Church Attendance* (Nashville: Abingdon Press, 1988).

2. A discussion of the changing context for ministry can be found in Lyle E. Schaller, *It's a Different World!* (Nashville: Abingdon Press, 1987).

Chapter Seven

1. Several suggestions on terminating a pastorate can be found in the final chapter of Lyle E. Schaller, *The Pastor and the People,* rev. ed. (Nashville: Abingdon Press, 1986).

2. This point is developed in great detail in Robert H. Frank, *Choosing the Right Pond: Human Behavior and the Quest for Status* (New York: Oxford University Press, 1985).